A STILL
UNTITLED
(NOT QUITE)
AUTOBIOGRAPHY

A STILL UNTITLED (NOT QUITE) AUTOBIOGRAPHY

BY

RON MOODY

JR
BOOKS

Special thanks to my super-perceptive, ever-patient editor Liz Rose (such taste . . . such discernment . . .); to my friend and publisher over many years, Jeremy Robson, whose support, enthusiasm and input made all the difference; and to his astonishingly efficient assistant Jessica Feehan, who not only conquered the mysteries of my antique computer and my scribbled scrawl but kept me going with chocolate digestive biscuits.

First published in Great Britain in 2010 by
JR Books, 10 Greenland Street, London NW1 0ND
www.jrbooks.com

The author would personally like to acknowledge the photograph by Lord Snowdon on page 9, the photograph by Rafael on page 14 and the drawing by Osbert Lancaster on page 8, which have been a prized part of his collection for more years than he cares to remember. And a big thanks to Vivienne Martin for the photographs on pages 12 and 13. Alan Davidson p.16; *Daily Mail*/ Rex Features p. 2 (top right); Dezo Hoffmann/Rex Features p.11; Everett Collection/Rex Features p.15 (bottom); Popperfoto/Getty Images p.10; Hulton Archive/Getty images p.13 (bottom)

ISBN 978-1-907532-11-5

1 3 5 7 9 10 8 6 4 2

Printed by MPG Books Ltd, Bodmin, Cornwall

To my own lovely Therese and our own lively cast,
Catherine, Daniel, Matthew, Michael, Jonathan and Conrad

Contents

Adventures In Enigma, Truth, Serendipity, Paradox And Show-Biz

Enigma e-nig'-ma, n. (L. *oenigma*, from Gk *ainigma*, to speak darkly, from *ainos*, a tale) A dark saying, in which something is concealed under obscure language; a riddle; something containing a hidden meaning which is proposed to be guessed; a person whose conduct or disposition is inexplicable.

Truth trooth, n. (A. Sax. *treowthe* from *treowe*, true) The state or quality of being true; conformity to fact or reality; veracity. The correspondence between a proposition and the fact, situation, or state of affairs that verifies it.

Serendipity serran-dippitti, n. (Coined in 1754 by Horace Walpole after the heroes of the Persian fairy tale *The Three Princes of Serendip* [ancient name for Sri Lanka]. Tendency or ability of prepared mind to make lucky discoveries by 'happy' accident. That happy blend of wisdom and luck by which something is discovered not quite by accident. Finding 'A' while looking for 'B', or in 'C' instead of 'D'.

Paradox par'a doks, n. (Gk. *paradoxon*, from *para*, beyond, and *doxa*, opinion) A statement which appears to be at variance with common sense, or to contradict some previously ascertained truth, though when properly investigated, it may be perfectly well-founded.

Showbiz shõ-biz, n. (New York shõ-biz'ness, from Ger. *schauen*, to exhibit or present to view; clever words, great legs, catchy tunes, make big bucks, go bust. There's no business like it.)

Prelude:

Memory Man, 1940

1940. The second year of World War II.

The boy was about sixteen. He had a wash of spring greens about the gills, boasting a wealth of inexperience and self-doubt. Never done this before, well, only inside his locked bedroom, entirely by himself, facing the wardrobe mirror, singing *Cleaning Windows* along with George Formby on the Ferguson music centre, followed by Formby's brilliantly punctuated *plonks* and *puddly-dum-dums* on the uke. The boy had all that off to a tee, practising finger-rolls every day on his bus ticket in the back seat of the bus on his way to school. *Plunk-a-dunk-a-diddly-dunk-a-diddly-diddly-dunka-dunka!* Disregarding suspicious stares from passing bus conductor.

Never done it because he never had the nerve, so what was he doing now at a local talent contest in Allison Hall, the old red-brick Victorian Church Hall in Green Lanes, Haringey? Never done it before but something he would never forget, he was painfully, definitely *backstage*, so somehow he had managed to fiddle himself into the local talent show, probably because all the young men were in the war, only the grizzle-chinned old 'uns and the bum-fluffed young 'uns were free to appear! He was pretty good at playing the uke like George, pretty good at screwing up his eyes like George, singing in high-pitched Lancashire like George, *very* good at the *plunk-diddly-plunk-dunk* like George, so what was wrong with him being there, ukulele in hand – well, banjolele in hand (a banjolele is shaped like a banjo, a ukulele is shaped like a guitar), scrupulously tuned to *'my dog has fleas' (A-D-Fsharp-B)*, standing in the wings, waiting to go on and stop the show cold like George with *When I'm Cleaning Windows*?

Nothing wrong at all. Except for some reason, he didn't remember anybody else being backstage, it all seemed totally deserted! It was still deserted when the moment arrived! The boy stepped on. Deep, dark silence! He walked to the centre and turned. Hell! He was blinded by spotlights spouting lava, couldn't see a thing in the great cavern of darkness beyond, not even the monsters that certainly lurked there, and bought tickets. Absolutely no sign of any audience! Was he facing the wrong way? Was it all a dream?

He stood there, sixteen years old, a teenage ukulele virtuoso, about to stop the show! It was time to begin! He tried to release his breath but it was lodged in his throat. That's when he went deaf. Oddly enough, he didn't feel *too* faint. Because something was telling him again, it was time to begin!

He plunked his opening riff, *Plunk diddly plunk plunk, plunk, plunk, plunk*! Again! *Plunk diddly plunk plunk, plunk, plunk, plunk*!

He had the impression that he had begun to sing.

> *Now I go cleaning windows*
> *To earn an honest bob . . . plunk a plunk*!

And then he dried. Stone cold dead in de market! Remembered nothing! Not a word! He stood there looking at the invisible audience for some time, and he imagined they were looking at him, but they made no sound, not even a derisive raspberry to cheer him on. Nothing! *Was* he dreaming it? Maybe it was *their* dream? He turned and walked off in complete silence. He didn't remember any more. Maybe they dreamed each other?

Part One

Praise But Not Quite Personal

1

Truth

The mysterious events which I am about to set before you (as Sir Arthur Conan Doyle, sleuth-monger and advocate, might so nicely have put it) began in the autumn of 2001, when I was invited by the Oxford Stage Company to play the part of veteran comedian, Eddie Waters, in Trevor Griffiths' masterpiece *Comedians*.

I'd seen the play in its original run at the National Theatre at the Old Vic in September, 1975, 26 years earlier, with Jimmy Jewel cast right down to his roots as Eddie, the retired comedian, teaching local evening classes in comedy to as wild an assortment of racist, sexist, homophobic pupils as any racist, sexist, homophobic audience could hope to sigh for.

Jimmy Jewel was the funny half of Jewel and Warriss, the biggest stars on radio and in Variety after World War II. Then TV took over and revealed that Jimmy's funny voice came from an equally life-crumpled face. His heavy Northern accent was loaded with baffled Mancunian squawks of sublime innocence – *izzay?* – *dozzay?* When the act broke up Jimmy astonished us again by going it alone as a really fine actor. Jimmy brought his own Truth to Eddie. He knew where he came from. He knew what made him tick. But the play demanded more. Eddie has an awful secret. He wants to do good. And this burning zeal to reform society is not explained until his final gut-wrenching scene with the rebel student, Price. Only then do we understand why he must perforce wage a war of wit and guile against his own pupils, his fame-hungry novices, clinically wielding his cerebral scalpel to analyse, satirize and vaporize jokes that hate women, degrade sex and feed on prejudice. Only then do we understand why he is concerned to nurture only the *true* joke of the thinking *comedian*, never the prejudiced jibe of the down-market *comic*.

According to Trevor Griffiths, 'a *true* joke, a comedian's joke, has to do more than release tension, it has to liberate the will and the desire; it has to change the situation'. In a word, make us look hard at ourselves and do something about it! Change today into tomorrow! True enough, but here I'm afraid I have to question whether this kind of Utopian social comment can come from material dreamed up by individual comics whose concern for their fellow man ends with a neurotic need for thirty minutes of well-milked filth. Change comes more from comedy writers who have the foresight and intellect to raise standards and generally to elevate the winds of change *above* the belt. We had this in the satirical theatre revues of the Fifties, the urbane Globe Revues, the chic Royal Court series, and particularly in the hilarious, rumbustious output of Peter Myers, Alec Grahame and Ronnie Cass, culminating in *For Amusement Only* where the closing scena, *The Vagabond Student*, was notorious for sending the ladies out of the theatre with mascara streaming down their cheeks. Here was social satire in its highest form; amateur dramatics would never be the same again. Here was a *true* joke to please Trevor, here was *Truth* a-plenty, albeit a special case, the Truth of Social Comment. The Truth that is reiterated in the final scene of *Comedians* where Eddie tells Price what he thinks of his grotesque variety act:

WATERS   It was ugly. It was drowning in hate. You can't change today into tomorrow on that basis. You forgot a thing called . . . the Truth.

PRICE   The truth. Can I say . . . look, I wanna say something. What do you know about the truth, Mr Waters? You think the truth is beautiful? You've forgotten what it's like. You knew it when you started off . . . you knew it then all right. Nobody hit harder than Eddie Waters, that's what they say. Because you were still in touch with what made you . . . hunger, diphtheria, filth, unemployment, penny clubs, means tests, bed bugs, head lice . . . Was all that truth beautiful? Truth was a fist you hit with. Now it's like . . . now it's like cowflop, a day old, hard until it's underfoot and then it's . . . green, soft. Shitten.

So much for the *Truth of Social Comment*. Telling it as it is. The wake-up call! But remember, only a special case, there is much more to it, and we will encounter many other kinds of Truth.

Patience, patience, we'll find them soon enough.

We rehearsed in the Lower Hall of St Andrew's and Upstream Church in Short Street, branching off the Cut where the Young Vic squats.

Several trendy restaurants had raised the tone of the area since I played there in Byron's *Marino Faliero*. The one I found most inviting was I think Italian-Thai, maybe Singapore-Greek, definitely Oriental-Occidental and indisputably foreign. A sweet-faced Hindu- type lady beamed out of the window. She was wearing some kind of dark black, air hostess style uniform, which suggested she was some sort of maitresse d'. I looked at the inviting polyglot menu, switched to her inviting smile, smiled at the menu, smiled back at her smile and could not resist either. I walked through the door of the crowded restaurant, smiled my way up to her and said,

'Do you have a table?' and she smiled back and said, 'I'm sorry, we are full up' without moving a muscle. She was still smiling invitingly as I slunk out, watched by dozens of well-fed, smiling diners, wondering why she would bother to lure me in just so she could throw me out. I lunched thereafter in an unsmiling Pizza Express, a giant mankind-step downwards along The Cut, but a perfect spot to swot my lines.

The Lower Hall was large enough to take the six desks that made up the set, with Eddie's desk on a dais at the upper end but with barely enough room at the lower end for a director, a stage manager, a dialogue coach (in au-then-ti-cal-laay accented Mancunian), or anyone else, including the author, who happened to drop by and didn't mind standing.

The director, Sean Holmes, was a sturdy young giant with a boxer's build, T-shirt, jeans and biceps that discouraged argument. Not that he argued with anyone, or punched anyone for that matter. If you had an idea he didn't like, he didn't actually reject it, he just didn't tell it to the other actors and, starved of support, it quietly faded away. Like the time I found the 'pupils' didn't react quickly enough to Eddie's commands, thereby reducing his authority. I mentioned it to Sean. He didn't disagree. But he didn't tell the 'pupils'. So I persisted, suggesting that perhaps Eddie, who had the style to be a spare-time football referee, could blow a whistle to command attention. He didn't disagree. But he didn't tell the 'pupils'. So when I blew the whistle, nobody reacted. I gave up and went back to shouting at deaf 'pupils'. Let *them* motivate.

Sean spoke only of the play. His method of directing was intensive, a relentless, repetitive, brain-hammering stream of consciousness, over and over and over, informing us what we had done after each run, as if we didn't know. He never seemed to be satisfied or dissatisfied. He was a drill sergeant and we were being drilled. But he did suggest valuable bridging touches that opened up lines and links to action.

And on the first night, his methods paid off; we performed impeccably, too brainwashed to even think about nerves. It was clear he had his own grand design for the play, he seemed to know exactly where he was going, we were encouraged to trust him. So what was puzzling me?

Here it comes! The first hint of something new, the first hint of an Enigma; the first flickerings of mystery in the air. Nothing cheerful and exciting to enliven rehearsals, like a severed head stuffed in the Lower Hall closet, just simply something not . . . quite . . . all there. That comes of using the word! Enigma! A curious word with various enigmatic meanings, not least that it is a darkish saying in which something is concealed beneath! Popular usage might go for a 'dark side'. Although some prefer 'riddle' or hint at 'legerdemain'.

Anyway, there we were, rehearsing well enough, an amiable bunch enjoying the exercise, going all the way with eye contact, playing to each other, finding the meanings of the words, establishing relationships, getting to know the mix of characters, all good stuff in the early stages of any rehearsal, in that all-devouring search for truth in performance.

There it is again! Another truth! Truth in Performance, which of course must include Truth of Character, Truth of Dialect, how about the Truth of Sub-text, and later on the Truth of Costume and the Truth of Setting? You may well protest that I digress too much on the many paths of boring old Truth when I was just about to lead you up a mysterious, exciting path to a young Enigma. To which I protest, dare we not digress when we are seeking the solution to an Enigma which may well have its roots in one of these kinds of Truth? And isn't it as good a time as any to put the question that Pontius Pilate failed to answer two thousand years ago . . . 'What is Truth?'

Truth, coming up so many times in Trevor's play, the main bone of contention between Eddie and his iconoclastic pupil, Price, that way up front in rehearsal I had to pin it down, defy the mighty methodologist, Karl Popper, and dare to define it, then write it on the front of my script! First, a heavy dictionary definition: 'Truth . . . the property implicitly attached to a proposition by belief in or assertion of it'.

Well, that's no better than sterile solipsism, *Cogito ergo sum*, Descartes and Bishop Berkeley telling us that thinking makes it so. To claim a play is truthful because the writer and director believe in it leads to situations where the actor protests: 'You forgot a thing called . . . the Truth! I am playing a gentle priest, how can I, in all truth, kill the penitent slave?' and the director says: 'Because it's in the script!' or 'Because I say so!', or, if he's a really erudite and companionable fellow, 'Because I believe it and because I assert it and because – shut up and kill the bastard!'

Let's try another definition:

'Truth . . . correspondence between a proposition . . . and the fact, situation or state of affairs that verifies it.'

Surely, that is more the truth we seek, truth set in objective observation and independent record, in a verifiably real world. We check it out, we research the facts, we chain our Beliefs and Assertions to the railings of Truth embedded in the concrete of Reality. Even that won't give us the Big One, Absolute Truth, but it's as good as it gets for our finite, pygmy minds.

Digression over, back once more to the Enigma and those first few flickerings of mystery. There was nothing unusual about the general air of approval, with perhaps even a hint of blind optimism in the room. After all it was (we believed) a brilliant play, and we were heading (we believed) for the West End, after a brief (we knew) provincial run with (we believed, as do we actors not all believe) an exemplary cast. Which said, was not the smug bubble of vanity it might seem, considering it included Martin Freeman, from the much vaunted TV series, *The Office*, and *The Hitchhikers Guide to the Galaxy*; as well as the then barely known David Tennant, soon to be hailed in *Dr Who* as one of the finest occupants of the Tardis (and the front page of the *Radio Times*), and let us not forget George Leyton, from *Doctor in the House*, who was right on the ball as the toxic Simon Cowell of the talent-spotting showcase, and come to think of it, I wasn't so bad myself!

But why was there no *personal praise*? At least from the director? There were of course, no critics yet, no audiences to give us the good word, a morsel of fulsome flattery to get us through the day. Nobody said 'You were great!', 'Terrific!', 'My gosh, you were fantastic!', 'Excuse me while I get off my knees!' – the humbler of the norms for personal praise. Nobody even sneaked in an oft and well deserved 'Lousy!' to give us at least a level. That didn't suit me, I like to know where I'm at! Of course, we all know that if a pro tells you you're 'great' that means you're 'good', if he says you're 'good', that means 'don't give up the day job'. Just pray that he never says you're 'interesting'. No matter, we have learned to keep our feet on the ground, grade down the encomiums, pick up on the plus signs, and play the game of theatrical-rhetorical. And if nobody says nothing, who cares if that's a double negative?

Actually, to be fair and appear to contradict myself far too soon, somebody did say something. On the rare occasions when Trevor Griffiths came by for a masterclass in comedy we did enjoy a little personal praise. He said we were the best cast he'd seen in his play. Although he said that while we were still on the book, so he could have meant we were getting his words right, but I really think he almost meant we were the best. Either way, from that kindly, clever man, it was what we needed. I've always said there are two kinds of bores. Those who don't know and talk. And those who know and don't talk. Well Trevor knew and talked and illuminated and – maybe most important of all – encouraged. He just didn't come round often enough. And maybe writers don't count!

And it was early days, we had a long way to go. Working as an actor, I try to make an appraisal of present performance as a percentage of potential. I rated rehearsals of *Comedians* at forty percent. So I worked on steadily, fixing lines and moves and accent, not really deserving praise or giving it for that matter, and obviously over-reacting to the pressure of rehearsal. Nonetheless, that tiny frisson of puzzlement remained firmly lodged at the back of my very busy tiny mind.

The Enigma beckons . . . as Eddie Waters in Trevor Griffiths', *The Comedians*.

2

Enigma

The puzzlement blossomed, took on a hint of frustration but stayed within the bounds of optimism when we opened the play in Exeter. The lovely little Northcott Theatre graces a university campus worthy of Capability Brown.

I have to admit it, I'm a sucker for universities. When I'm in Los Angeles, I gravitate towards Westwood, in Dublin I wander round Trinity . . . Edinburgh, Glasgow, Oxford, Cambridge, you name it, I'll find it, it's like coming home. In London, on theatrical or any other business, I seem to be always somewhere within a mile of Senate House. I love those great buildings and open spaces with hundreds of students milling around, those immeasurably lucky young people with the world before them and all the intellectual ladders they need to climb to the top! It's always been my world as much as Show Business has been my life, and when the two come together, as in Exeter, I am doubly blessed.

The Northcott opening was good. Sean's direction, as I said, brainwashed us into a first night free of nerves. I was confident yet not without a tinge of anxiety, for I had qualms about drying on some of the long, didactic speeches, the savage stabs of imagery in counterpoint, that Trevor must have taken wicked delight in writing for whoever played Eddie. I did indeed go blank a couple of times, but, with a skill fine-tuned from a lifetime of lousy memory, turned the lapses into dramatic pauses. Then, by the kindest of miracles, or the subtlest of prompts (bless you, Martin Freeman, muttering my cues as if you were talking to yourself!) the words popped back into my head. Otherwise it was like a student sitting for an exam and wondering how those ice-veined inquisitors-cum-critics, lurking like basking sharks in the cold, dank, darkness of the auditorium, were going to mark our cards. After all, a first night is *exactly* like an examination with the critics, *exactly* like examiners, telling us if we've passed, got an A+ or failed, with the glorious difference that we, unlike examinees, get to do it all again! And if the critics are responsible, perceptive, and guide us well, and are not out to make their own names by lamentably well-written character assassinations, we can put it right before we get to town.

But the Enigma, waiting in the wings, was about to take its quirky bow. There were drinks on the Oxford Stage Company after the show, in the front of house bar. Sean Holmes said 'What do you think?'; Dominic Dromgoole, the Artistic Director and now A.D. of the Shakespeare Globe, smiled and nodded wisely. But these were merely perfunctory in-group greetings, the thing to do when you've shared four weeks of hard graft and got the damned thing on. No, the enigmatic point was that not one member of the theatre staff, backstage crew or audience gave me a single word of personal praise. I don't know if they praised the others, I was too busy wondering what I'd done wrong! I wasn't on top of the lines yet, true. And yes, I knew from experience that I was usually bordering on 50% potential on a first night, and had a way to go. But I'd just been on the boards of the living theatre, God help me, and nobody seemed to notice I was there! Come to think of it, nobody seemed to notice anyone was there. And pros need to be told!

Mid-week, Vernon Duker, an old school mate of mine, now owner of the Palace Hotel, Torquay and a huge estate on the cliffs overlooking Brixham Harbour, came to see me with his colleague, Max, and a very attractive lady. Vernon and I were in the same class at the Hornsey County School, so we each knew exactly how old the other was and when you know that you have to stay friends. I'd always said he should have been an actor, he had the looks and bearing of the Duke of Wellington and would have ended up owning the Theatre Royal, Drury Lane. He'd driven up to see me twice before, when I was appearing at the Northcott in musical versions of *Sherlock Holmes* and *The Canterville Ghost*, and his appraisal of my work as Holmes and the Spook had been very fair, very accurate, and *very* flattering. Opinions like that deserve *respect*! Hardly surprising that I now awaited his consummate opinion.

He said nothing. He wasn't that impressed with the play, didn't think it would go into the West End although that was the firm intent of the management, and because I knew and trusted him so well, I chatted on and waited patiently for the good word on *me*. It didn't come. Fair enough. He'd taken the trouble to drive all the way from Torquay, a lifelong friend and an honest man is entitled to his lousy opinion. But when he compounded his felonious comments by grossly over-praising an actor he had seen in town, that did it! 'What about my character?' I said sweetly. 'Is it working?' Instant head-nodding and kind remarks all round. Of course! I was always very good! ('Very good' in theatrical-rhetorical means 'competent'.) Max was pleasantly surprised to find I was playing the lead, since I wasn't billed above the title and I had a postcard-sized photo out front. I explained that the Oxford Stage Company, in the best rep tradition, just loved all that ensemble, egalitarian, 'names in alphabetical order' stuff, and I was as puzzled as he why my agent hadn't sent a 10" × 8"! Generally speaking not what I'd hoped for, but friendship secured, *gaudeamus igitured*, and the impeccable Vernon gave me a lift back to the Queen's Hotel in his state-of-the-art, fully electronic, virtually self-driving, critically bloody flawless, 'very good' car.

The next jolly moment of puzzlement came when Suli, my former dresser on *The Canterville Ghost* and now promoted to the Northcott front of house, came to see the show. We met in the Circle Bar later and her lovely face wore an untypical frown. Where was my *smiling* Suli, morale-booster and Patron Saint of insecure actors? She kept insisting I should be angrier in the last scene, match David Tennant's ferocity as Price, the iconoclastic clown with that ugly, savage and utterly tasteless stand-up routine in Act II. A local review, which mostly concerned itself with the play and the direction, said, almost as an after-thought: *'Ron Moody and David Tennant go for the jugular'*. I didn't quite understand that and I didn't understand Suli. Was she trying to tell me something? Then why not *tell* it? She said she would be in the following night and look at it again. The following night, I gave what I felt was a bigger performance, got very ferocious in the last scene, whaddyerthinkerthat, Suli? She didn't even come backstage. Whatever I was doing wrong, I was still doing.

After Exeter, the brief tour finished with a week at the Oxford Playhouse. I stayed, as always, at the dear old Randolph Hotel, a few minutes from the theatre along Beaumont Street.

The room was excellent, who could argue with a four-poster, a bowl of fruit and a box of Belgian chocolates shaped like a mortarboard? But somebody had destroyed the great restaurant, divided it into three with an over-lit oyster bar hogging one end, an under-lit extension to the public bar slicing off the other, whilst the once magnificent main restaurant lurked miserably middle-lit between with most of its tables heaped, for some reason, in the centre.

I think this obsession with change is a new disease, Managerius Makismarkus, picked up in the supermarkets. Six weeks under a new Manager and shelves are stripped out, walls torn down, and every item from fruit and veg to sauces and dips wrenched heartlessly from its comfortably familiar place, while the new Manager watches it all on his CCTV, cackling 'That's the way to make your mark!' Then Managerius Makismarkus progresses to the final, pitiful stage where the Manager is given a golden hand-tremble, promoted to Head Office, somebody else comes in store and does it all again, and a few years later, Lord help us, our man turns up running the Randolph!

The opening night at the Oxford Playhouse was very good. No vain pretences here, just simple fact, we did – *I* did – a very good – very well run-in – opening night. I felt generally better about the whole play, the big speeches had settled in, I was performing them with more pace and a lot more Truth (in Performance, Character, Dialect, Sub-text, Costume and Setting), finding the light and shade, trying still, with surprising difficulty, to build the humour in Eddie, discovering his comedic stage persona, as is the case with most professional comedians, pretty well in the man himself. And remember, we were in Oxford! No offence to lovely university campus Exeter, but this was sophisticated *Oxford* and I was sophisticated LSE, this crowd had an intellectual buzz to it and these were *my* people, tonight must be *mine*, kudos will be mine, I shall make a grand yet discreet after-show entrance into the front-of-house bar and modestly await . . . .the plaudits!

'Thank you for coming,' said the young lady with the very pretty face, introduced to me as the Artistic Director of the Playhouse. 'Thank you for coming,' said a middlish-aged man oozing gravitas whom, I suspected – because nobody felt he needed introduction – was the Administrator of the Playhouse. I had no idea what linked the Oxford Stage Company to the Oxford Playhouse except that there were now more nice people making me wonder if I'd been on stage that

night. I saw Sean who said 'What do you think?'; Dominic
Dromgoole smiled from afar and looked wise; somebody
handed me a drink and I sipped it and stared at all the backs.

'Thank you for coming.' That was *it*? The sum total of
communal comment on my work, my skill, my dedication,
not a word *of* me, *for* me (or *by* me for that matter), not one
single individual, personal note of praise for a forcefully
spoken, well-researched, Manchester-accented, old-time
comedian-cum-teacher played with panache and fifty years of
comedic experience by an actor of sufficient standing in the
profession to deserve more than 'Thank you'? 'Thank you', for
all that? 'Thank you', incidentally, which, in theatrical-
rhetorical, means 'Don't call us, we'll call you'?

Where, by Exeter, Oxford and St George, did I go wrong?

3
Personal Praise

Now, wait, wait, wait a minute! Let us bring this whole thing into perspective! Where is the big *Enigma* here, where is there mystery compelling enough to write a book? What is wrong with a nice little 'Thank you'? Surely a flattering expression of gratitude for the devotion of one's graciously given and grossly underpaid time and talent to the cultivation of Oxford's precious, if parochial, little cabbage patch of a theatre? Forgive me if there is a hint of pique here bubbling up through the cracks! A frisson of the fulminatory finger! What does the Moody fellow want? Personal Praise? Theatrical hyperbole? Gushing ol' luvvie chat? Hasn't he heard of ensemble playing, company spirit, teamwork, pulling together, sharing the limelight, play up, play up, and play their game? The other actors in *Comedians* certainly upheld the company way. In fact, when I ventured to share my puzzlement with them, they were genuinely surprised. What was wrong with having the whole production praised instead of yourself? After all, in praising the whole, you are clearly praising the parts! Was there a hint in their company voice that it was time to face myself, an egomaniac, has-been, so-called star, clutching at the fading limelight before it disappeared entirely? That may well be.

But after fifty years, you learn a thing or two. (Who said that

line? Or rather, who over seventy hasn't said that line?) You
learn that if people come backstage and talk about the set, as
they used to after Lionel Bart's *Blitz*, if people come backstage
and bring a message from Cousin Perry, as most of my
relatives do anyway, if people do *not* come backstage at all,
even to insult you to your face or slap it with a glove – in a
word, if you do not get your own private portion of personal
praise after a show and that same praise night after night –
then you have quite simply, to descend from the oracular by
the funicular to the vernacular, *missed the boat*!

The incomparable Tommy Cooper, prognathous cackle and
all, used to get painfully close to the truth of this theatrical
roller-coaster.

'If you do your act, go well, you know, tear 'em up,'
breathed the great crag jaw, 'they all come round backstage.'
Here he mimed standing at his dressing room door, receiving
guests, smiling, sighing, shaking scores of hands. 'Thank you.
Thank you very much. Haha. Bless you. Thank you. Ha.
Lovely. Thank you. Was I? How kind. Yes. Thank you. Haha.
Hahaha. (Pause) But if you don't do well, die on y' feet, you
know, miss the boat, hahaha!' Here he mimed standing again
at his dressing room door, watching a visitor approaching.
Tommy raises his hand for shaking, a huge beam of hope
stretches from chin to massive brow, the grin stays as the
visitor comes level, fades sharply as the visitor goes past,
leaving Tommy staring endlessly after the disappearing
figure, hand still outstretched, with an expression of trouser-
dropped, egg-in-the-hat chagrin which could only find
harbour in that fjord he called a face.

So this is no peacock tail of petty ego, no precocious child
snivelling to be the centre of attention, no lonely misfit seeking approval, or ethnic outsider seeking social acceptance, but
the recognition that the blessed gifts of talent, skill, star
quality and indeed the ability to achieve anything in the
theatre, must be praised by others, and thereby encouraged to

grow by others! How else, dear Quintus Roscius Gallus, Actor of Actors, can even one so great know his worth? The irony is that on stage you are at your most vulnerable. On film you see 'rushes', on TV you have monitors, but on stage you are, literally, blind. You need eyes out front – the practised and hopefully informed eye of the director, the personal and hopefully prejudiced eye of family and friends, the professional and hopefully unprejudiced eye of the critic, and the all-seeing, all-paying and hopefully 'House Full' eye of the Box Office! Only with their help – praise – can you find the courage to suppress your fears and rise to your heights!

As for ensemble playing, much as I admire the concept of a pure and selfless denial of personal ambition in the name of creative fellowship, and much as I love to see any such evidence of the better side of man's nature, I fear it is as transparent as the Emperor's New Clothes, concealing nothing. In the acting profession, there is only intense rivalry, metamorphosed into the 'luvviest' collaboration by mutual necessity and a saccharine desire to be loved by one's peers. For the rivers of rivalry run deep, the talents aren't equal, the parts aren't matched, the manager wants a hit, the director wants his mates, the public wants its favourites, and a star is a star is a *star*. Which, of course, if they look themselves in the eye and face the truth therein, is what *everybody* in and out of show business wants to be, and for more than fifteen minutes. 'I just wanna be a good actor?' Eeeeeeeeyargh! Who said that?

This does not mean, I hasten (I hasten hastily and emphatically) to add, that I am some kind of misanthropic, cynical actor-hater, I have had the most wonderful, fun-loving companions in all the musicals and revues and cabarets I have been privileged to be in, and I have no problems with straight players, even with those Shakespearian actors, who hide their pretensions and lack of truth behind the stylised chant and verbal regurgitations of Elizabethan dialogue. You can keep your Fourth Wall if you really want it, but to me, the true theatrical is always the man who loves his audience and wants them to know that he knows they are there. What you might call 'cocking an eye at the gods'. Remember A.E. Matthews? His audiences adored him, whether touring in World War 1 with Dame Marie Tempest or appearing in Carry On films without losing his dignity; carefully seated just off centre stage, somehow, whichever way he looked, facing the audience, his quiver bursting with devastating shafts of wit that hit the mark every time and set the audience of virtual 'cronies' in a roar! They were 'his people' and they knew he was there for *them*! But he never came out of character! What came over was not egotism or 'thinking he was funny' but simply and truly that he loved them! And wanted a little back. And here's a jolly Paradox, in that that, my friends, is very much the way to play Shakespeare – remember Olivier in *Richard III*, that twinkle in the eye? – but let's leave it for another book, another time. Indeed, it may well be why Personal Praise means so much to me. So let us get back to finding where it went.

4

Serendipity

The week at Oxford was nearly over. I had tried variation after variation to no effect. The solution could be under my nose, yet just as likely in a place I'd never dreamt of! *Insufferable Enigma, show yourself! Speak to me! I can take it*!

After all, it wasn't the first time I'd opened in a show and faced the possibility that I wasn't any good, that any success I'd had to date was no more than a fortuitous freak, that nobody had the heart to tell me, and that my profit on presuming to flaunt myself in public was to endure the purgatory of these belly-chilling enigmas of the actor's craft! Knowing that these torments would keep coming with every show, with every part, with frightening regularity! Afraid that this one might be the ultimate, insoluble enigma! But knowing that, by hook or by crook, it was somehow going to get cracked!

We-e-e-ell, it's the fun of the g-a-me! The brain play bit! Because, at such moments of impasse the academic mind sluices back to its sources, finds itself at a confluence of experiences, influences, and an awesome number of times the same thing has happened before, the solution has been found, and then – ludicrously – forgotten! (Now there's a *true* joke, Trevor! We of short memory keep learning the same lessons!)

So in a career of hits and misses there was no reason to think that this Enigma would prove any different. I'd been rounding up the usual subjects, asking myself the usual questions: 'Was the character well-conceived and rounded, was the movement thereby sharp and set, the voice thereby articulated, the energy up?', since each or all of them might be to blame, and work on one or all might put it right.

But not this time! I worked on one and all but there was still something missing! Was it in me? Was it on stage? Was it the audience? Was it the play? Was it everything? That's when I began to think there was something *else* involved, that's when the Enigma began to really chill the atmosphere, in and out of the theatre. It's hard to describe that feeling when a show isn't working. You wake up with the sense of defeat in your stomach, you carry that lump of misery through the day and into the theatre, you slap on make-up, and drag on costume, and do the show and still it doesn't work until the last scene and that works and makes it worse because you don't know why, and all the director can say is: 'What do you think?' So in the end you really have to do something! In the end, it is time to really stop and really think. It is time, in fact, to dig deeper. And that means we are confronting at last the Truth of Truths, the Truth of Causality. The Truth of Why. The Truth of what makes things *tick*. The dig down deep, oblique and lateral Truth of Scientific Method! Another ball game!

The Methodology of Science is a solid old house, but if the windows won't open to let in the light, we have to check the brickwork, if the bricks are off kilter, we probe the foundations! And where better to probe than the foundations of my very own theatrical career, those early formative years when I ventured into the fearsome terrain of the brave new world of entertainment, jumped feet first into all its jolly temptations and dangers, braved the battlegrounds of theatre, cabaret and one-night stands, the minefields of agents and critics, the cut and thrust of rivalry and competition, and, in a word, got my feet wet in what my father called so drily, 'the rat-race'! Those are the days when I was lucky enough to make every mistake known to man and learn from most of them, and naive enough to uncover every possible Enigma and recognise none of them!

So if we look back at a selection of significant experiences that beckoned me, wide-eyed, into 'the rat-race' (which, I have reason to believe, I know, qua Sociologist, better than most) we will surely find clues to my very own infuriating little Enigma, clues that will be there in every meaningful digression into biographical tit-bit, theatrical anecdote, career move up or down but hopefully never out, of my first seven years in show business. All you have to do is spot the clues! Keep your eyes open and your wits sharp, and see if you can suss out the solution.

And here is where – if I may lose my academic cool for a moment – it becomes exciting! We are in the Magic Land of Serendipity, oh, how I love that word! As you all know, it was invented by Horace Walpole in 1754, to describe a tendency or ability to make seminal discoveries by luck or accident, and I'd be likely to drag it in even if it didn't fit. But it does here! For in our quest, we may perhaps luckily discover not simply a solution to the laughable lack of Personal Praise in *Comedians*, the Enigma which triggered it all, but discover by lucky chance that there really was something else involved, something a little more all-embracing, something, perhaps, of which lack of Personal Praise was merely a part. We may even dare to hope for a jagged shard of inspiration to tear through the surface of the psychic crust and thrust up a monolithic Equation, one so challenging it may change our lives, one that might even claim to be a distant cousin of Einstein's $E = mc^2$! Not such an equation, God forfend, that it may bring down a city, but one, God bless us, that will bring down the house!

5

Diary

In looking back on those significant things that have in some way shaped my life and career, I must include keeping a diary since the age of sixteen.

I had a dentist who talked nonstop as he worked, never used anaesthetic, and counterpointed the merciless whine of the drill with jolly little quips such as: 'Now this is really going to hurt', or 'It's only pain', or 'That will remind you to come early!' I found it hard to laugh at his jokes with a drill in my gum, and when my nerves finally encouraged me to forget not only the time but the date of an appointment, he insisted I make a note of these diverting sessions in a diary. So I dutifully got a diary and wrote in all my appointments. The first was with my mother's second cousin, a gentle fellow who barely spoke as he worked, and practised painless dentistry.

The diary began as a small notebook noting lists of appointments, grew to add sketches and comments on the day, and expanded to a slim volume that progressed to a full commentary on events. I then began to buy elegant, day-to-a-page, leather-bound volumes from Letts and Smythsons and Harrods, believing in the magical probability that the finer the volume, the greater the events to be recorded therein, culminating in a magnificent, grained-leather tome with gold-plated clasp purchased at Gucci-New York where I had been brought by Columbia Pictures for the premiere of *Oliver!* in 1968. It was a loose-leaf diary, and when the first year was over I replaced the printed data with blank pages, allowing me to expand or reduce the amount written every day. In no time at all, I was writing 80,000 words a year. I can pretty well tell what happened to the hour and to the day for the last seventy years. But there is more to it than that.

There is a grand mystique to a diary that only diarists know. It is more than a chronological record of mundane events, it is a key that literally unlocks a door to the past. Every word on the page evokes its time, every paragraph is its world reborn, and there they are, all the days of your life, being lived again in the scribble of events as if they are actually happening up to seventy years after the moment of writing. Read a page and back come the minutest details of the day, the people, the places, the images, the feelings, the hopes, the fears, as near as you can get to total recall. You even remember the images you had to leave out to avoid a diary three times the size. Not to mention those particularly private moments and deeply dark thoughts that are best kept secret if you don't happen to be a Freud or a Strindberg.

There is no room here for the misremembered moment, the slip of a dozen years between memory and fact, which happens in practically every memoir written with no diary and no independent spatial and temporal research to back it up, and is thereby unable to guarantee yet another of those inescapable, but indispensable Truths, the Truth of Chronology. I shall prove this to you in some of the biographical illustrations by writing these moments firstly as I remember them, as clearly and vividly as any practised raconteur who dines out on memories souped up with ribald moments, sly embellishments and downright lies, to add the piquant taste of legend 'to an otherwise dull and unconvincing narrative'. I shall then, at the expense of my own credibility and in the few cases where these vividly clear 'memories' are way too far off track, follow them up with the brutal, black-and-white facts of what the diary says!

Part Two

Biography But Not Quite Boswell

1

Eternal Student

An Actor must work all his life, cultivate his mind, train his talents systematically, develop his character; he may never despair and never relinquish this main purpose – to love his art with all his strength and love it unselfishly.
Constantin Stanislavski, *Building a Character*

There speaks the Master. You don't just go to drama school, graduate, stop learning, become famous, make a fortune, marry Madonna, buy five hundred acres of England, and check out your progress thereafter in the gossip columns of *Hello* magazine. It's more fun than that. Quite simply, you stay a student all your life. You think and you train and you grow. All your life. And you try not to despair and even if you do you never, never, never, *never* give up! Absolutely! Total agreement. But does Stanislavski really expect his 'Ahk-tor' to love his art with *all* his strength when he must need a goodly portion of that for other things like wives, families, children and Income Tax? Does he expect his true 'Ahr-tist' to stay celibate? Or go quietly mad like Van Gogh? Or does he permit him to cope with the all-consuming exigencies of the creative arts yet keep a perspective on life, hopefully retaining some tiny semblance of savings and sanity? As the great Walter Matthau is reputed to have said, 'I was a dedicated actor until I had a heart attack. That's when I stopped being dead-icated and turned to comedy.'

Maybe I have this down-to-earth view of Show Business because I didn't go to a drama school to learn the rules, I went to the London School of Economics and Political Science and learnt to bend them. I didn't know then that in 1894 a Fabian Socialist called Henry Hutchinson shot himself dead in the best Commedia dell'Arte tradition, and left Ten Thousand Pounds, a fortune for those days, to Sidney Webb, who used it to found the LSE in Clare Market in 1895. Nor did I then know that Joseph Grimaldi, the great Regency Clown, was born on the site of Clare Market in 1778, or that I would one day write a musical about him and play the part of Joe because I didn't think his greatest song, printed in Richard Findlater's definitive biography, *Grimaldi, King of the Clowns*, was very funny. I mean, what's funny about a song called *Hot Codlins*, which are potatoes baked in their skins?

> *A little old woman her living she got*
> *By selling hot codlins, hot, hot, hot,*
> *And this little woman who codlins sold,*
> *Tho' her codlins were hot, she felt herself cold,*
> *So to keep herself warm, she thought it no sin,*
> *To fetch for herself*
> *A quartern of –*

At which same instant the crowd lifts off the roof with a huge shout of 'Gin!', followed by raucous laughter, followed by three more verses of the little old lady's saga, and *Hot Codlins* lasts into the 1890s, sixty years after Grimaldi's farewell, and I try it out seventy years after that to see if it still works and it *does*! And I think Henry Hutchinson and Joe Grimaldi are still around Clare Market some place, training clowns like me and politicians!

So, I went to LSE on an ex-serviceman's grant of £180 per

annum, a very tidy sum for my days, purely and simply because one of the four co-founders of the School, with Sidney and Beatrice Webb and Graham Wallas, was my intellectual catalyst, my creative Colossus, the Irish genius who baffled me with his paradoxes, dazzled me with his blinding wit, and above all inspired my Socialist heart with his mountain-peak perception of Society, his blinding insights into every aspect of religion, politics, war, peace and the living of life – George Bernard Shaw!

I had huddled over a cast-iron, coke-burning stove, one icy day in 1947, probably the worst frozen-up winter on record, in the Education Section of the RAF Maintenance Unit, Skellingthorpe, Lincolnshire, and read Shaw's *Man and Superman*. I had read it and read it and re-read it. I had also stammered to myself quite a lot, not merely because of the fearsome freeze but because – gauche and unaware – I was in the early stages of a primitive, pre-theatrical Enigma. 'H-h-how did he do that?' I shivered. 'How could any one man be so f-f-f-frighteningly clever?' I shook. 'Where did he get these w-w-wonderful, new, amazing ideas?' I breathed, drooling tiny stalactites down my cheeks like an ice-bound Dracula. It was one of the great c-cold moments of my life!

There was nothing else for it. The solution to this Enigma was surprisingly simple, I would merely have to be accepted at LSE, graduate with a spectacular First in Sociology and Social Psychology, the only subjects that could loft me up there amid the Shavian peaks, climb swiftly to a Professor-ship, write didactic, neo-Shavian plays in my lengthy vacations on the Riviera, change society and bring peace to the world. These, I would say, were pretty well the more modest of my youthful ambitions at that time – to become a great playwright and a disciple of Shaw, carry on the great man's work? Ends like that, I mused, would do. For the time being.

2

Part Time/Full Time

'Oh, no! No, no, no! Absolutely impossible!'

The Squadron Leader S.Ad.O. was against me at once even before he'd seen me. Which he never actually did, because from the moment I entered, his eyes had been fixed on the second button of my tunic.

'Oh, no, no, no! I can't see how you can possibly have full time off!' (Nor could I, but I was hopeful.) 'At this – er – London School of Economics?' He thought about it for a moment, and made himself very angry. I could tell because his eyes moved up to my first button. It occurred to me that if I provoked him enough, he might actually look me in the eye.

'I'll let you know about it!'

'Sir!' I left, unlooked at but without rancour because it was clear that this happy little haberdasher had never even heard of LSE. The Education Officer had, but he hadn't known what to suggest so he had referred me to the Squadron Leader. That same afternoon I was referred to the Commanding Officer (superior type – eyes on badge of hat) who couldn't give me full time off, but would see what the Education Officer had to suggest. After two trips round this Inner Circle somebody decided I could have some time off, but I must arrange my studies to take up as little RAF time as possible. So I spent my first term at LSE as an evening student based on RAF Hendon in Colindale.

It would have been much simpler if I'd been demobbed in time for the Michaelmas Term in October 1947, but the course of true life never runs smooth. So I spent my days in the Radar section at Hendon, doing DI's on Ansons, poodling around with Lucero and IIC, toying with impedances and rejector circuits, and cursing clots who switched the RX so the gain was duff; and my evenings at LSE, listening to Professors Robbins on Indifference curves, Blackburn on hyperaesthesia, Hinchliff on Buddhist Dhammapada, and wondering why the hell the lecturers couldn't speak plain English.

I moved from jargon to jargon, milieu to milieu, a marginal man on the fringe of two worlds, blurring together like an off-phase projector. I lived for the evenings, and, paradoxically, had more fun with the days. The Radar section had Ken and Dave, who were my close friends, LSE was a passing show of anonymous strangers; the RAF provided me with crosswords, NAAFI breaks, table tennis and the radio-set I never did build, LSE gave me wallflower evenings at Freshers' Dances, Union Meetings where I sat in awe as 'giants' spake, and a delicately nurtured inferiority complex. It was in the RAF that I saw a Jamaican bash a cook over the head with a vinegar bottle because he was refused more potatoes. LSE yielded no such happy moments.

Unless perhaps that cold October Sunday when I joined the LSE Boat Club and paddled out from Chiswick Boathouse in my first four. Eight arms and four oars punched the boat through the water at terrifying speed, I caught a crab, the boat heeled to one side, the oar thudded my ribs, and the purpose of the sport became alarmingly clear – to get back to the bank! As we did, I saw a lone rower swimming towards us like a drowned rat, pushing his upturned shell before him – and I never went again.

But I was at LSE – the only place of Higher Learning I had ever wanted to be! I was a guest in the house of Bernard Shaw and the Webbs, the Citadel where Harold Laski held court. And above all, I was a University Student! Part Time!

'Number, Rank, Name!'

'1894342, AC1, Moody, R., Corporal!'

'Age!'

'24, Corporal!'

'Sign that . . . that . . . that . . . that!'

'What's the date, Corporal?'

'12th January, 1948! It's yer demob day – twit!'

'Now come on, chaps!' A Flight Lieutenant with an insensitivity of cosmic proportions joshed us affectionately. 'Take your demob leave, chaps, then remember the old esprit de corps, chaps, and come back with the boys, chaps.'

We took our eyes from the top button of his tunic and plunged through a series of corridors and offices and hangars in a never-ending stream, picking up money and chits and sports jackets and pin-striped trousers, and seeing – oh, blessed moment! – our Release Books ripped and torn to pieces before our bewildered eyes. Free. Free! Oh, madness and joy! Freeeeeeee!

On January 14th, 1948, a magnificent new Birthday Briefcase from Proud and Happy Parents gleaming in my Proud and Happy Hand, I set off for LSE to begin my new life as a University Student! Full Time!

Part time, full time, in no time at all I was Alice in Wonderland! Wandering through warrens of classes and lectures and societies and seminars . . . Ah! There was the Dormouse, pretending to be Professor Ginsberg, there, the White Rabbit, disguised thinly as Lionel Robbins, and as for the Mad Hatter, why, he was everywhere, proliferating himself onto every lecture platform in the place, pouring out platitudes of garbled logic and gobbledegook to the wisely nodding heads of Them What Was In The Know – everyone, that is – except me

And of course, there were thousands of Cheshire Cats, smiling widely from afar and fading mysteriously when I came too close. When I discovered that if I kept very quiet, the Cheshire Cats would allow me to approach and listen to their conversations, I became an excellent listener, a master of the role of attentive audience. But if I was foolish enough to open my mouth and say one word, they would fade instantly about their business.

I lost the power of speech. The outrageous exhibitionist of the RAF, the buffoon of every barrack room, the Aneurin Bevan of every NAAFI from Hendon to Henlow. I was suddenly struck dumb! My syntax went to pieces and my sentences tailed off in mid-air. I was too busy listening to my own, thin, nasal voice, my own vulgar London accent, so damnably aware that everybody else spoke so *well*! I went to a public-speaking class, determined to cure my disability, the Cheshire Cats orated – and I listened. When I was finally forced to speak, the trapped Cheshires listened back – and stopped smiling.

It was about this time that I developed my Nod, a symbol of acquiescence in group discussions, the limit of my participation in group activity. It carried me through classes, lectures, Union meetings and Refectory debates with considerable dignity. I became a Wise Silent Nodder Who Understood All. For of course I did! I was intensely critical of Robbins and Marshall and Ginsberg and Hinchliff and Beales and Smellie, who continuously missed the points that were so laughably clear to me, *and* without having had to read any of their recommended books! For was I not already a Shavian Creative Evolutionist, a Radical Socialist, a Rationalist and a Very Clever Person to boot? I was overcome with admiration for the student at a Robbins lecture on Economic Analysis, who, when that learned Prof. warned us that the lecture would be sticky if we hadn't read Marshall, stood up, bowed, and walked out. Almost as good as the Jamaican and the vinegar bottle.

But I would probably have nodded my way through the next two years at LSE with no trouble, no loss of face and no degree, if I hadn't, one morning in February, taken my FIRST BIG STEP! I replied to an advertisement for the post of cartoonist on *Beaver*, the wall newspaper in The Three Tuns. Cartoons and cruel caricatures had been a happy hobby since childhood – I revelled in long noses, buck teeth and piggy eyes and drew and lost many friends in the process. A few days later I found a letter in my pigeon hole from 'Tiger' Standish, the Editor, to say my application was gratefully accepted and would I cover the Valentine Ball? Fee, a free 4/6d ticket! The offer was irresistible! I had a government grant of £180 per annum, lived at home and gave a pound a week to my very dear parents, and managed my LSE on two pounds a week. I covered the Ball, with cartoons and comments on the types of personalities present – LSE came out of it as the only college where all the men had bow legs and all the women had flat chests – and had the enormous pleasure of nipping down to The Three Tuns one lunchtime to find my piece prominently displayed on the *Beaver* notice-board – and surrounded by a swarm of flat-chested, bow-legged students. I had signed it, unobtrusively, 'Jumna Krash', and I skulked around for a few changes of audience, revelling in the joy I bought to their piggy eyes and reading it a few dozen times myself. 'Brilliant!' the Walrus said; 'Very very funny,' returned the Carpenter. I nodded.

From that day, I had (you should excuse the expression) function and status. I was 'Jumna Krash', the unobtrusive *Beaver* cartoonist and if you were nice to me I could put your face on my wall. I began to spend my spare time in the *Beaver* office and suddenly found myself in growing contact with the student élite – for the Union office was on the third floor. It wasn't long before I was asked to illustrate an article in *Clare Market Review,* the *printed* student periodical, edited by Val Sherman, iconoclast elect, egotist supreme, and already a brilliant journalist. Years later this former communist was to become speech writer to Margaret Thatcher, and then Sir Alfred Sherman. I viewed him with some awe because he used to stand up with great authority at climactic moments in the Union meetings – and speak! And he had made up his mind that I was a budding Daumier and was wasting my time reading Sociology and should be a political cartoonist on a national newspaper. How could I possible consider such an idea? I was devoted to the ideal of an academic life. I attended every lecture on the syllabus, took copious notes in my meticulously organised, precisely tabulated master file, and one day soon, I would read them all and understand them and assimilate them – if I could decipher them.

Like Mr Lewisham, I had a schedule of work, a plan of study. For a start, I got up every morning. It was never easy, now I was free of RAF discipline – perhaps I went to bed too late. It would have to stop! I *must* keep to my schedule, ten minutes of push-ups and exercises, half an hour of German translation before breakfast! No time now, but I would have to begin tomorrow! Definitely and absolutely, tomorrow! I rushed breakfast, took the tube to Holborn, jog-trotted along Kingsway, making small but significant gestures as I passed the RAF Recruiting HQ, all the time cursing my ineptitude and my idiotic, inexcusable unpunctuality! Late every morning! Late again for Robbins in the New Theatre, scribble, scribble, what *was* he on about, egad, the man was so tall, no wonder he talked above our heads, hahaha! Stigler! That was the answer! I must read Stigler's *Theory of Price* and all would be revealed – tomorrow! Definitely and absolutely tomorrow! No time now, I had to illustrate *Beaver* Hansard for Tiger and discuss drawings for *CMR* with Val. Anyway the

Easter vacation was upon us, and I would now positively get down to some real work on all subjects. Definitely and absolutely! And then I took my SECOND BIG STEP! I discovered the library!

I had dropped in a few times in the Lent Term, braving the caustic surveillance of the Guardians at the Gate who, brothers to Customs men and traffic wardens, always made you feel you had half the library stuffed up your jumper. I had a paper to write on Veblen and took out his superb *Theory of the Leisure Class.* And all at once, I realised I had been wasting my time only attending lectures last term. Here were all the words, written *down,* not flying blind over my head and being humped, half-heard, into my note-book. I was able to sit and read and study and read again and think and look at other readers and admire their legs and wonder what they were reading and read what I was reading and slowly, very slowly I was able – to learn!

To the half-trained mind, the first major textbook you read is close to Holy Writ – the tight-knit arguments, the force of the intellect behind them, these are overpowering and unassailable. It is not surprising that the Bible and Marx have had such power over the Peasant. The second book fills you with helpless panic, you blunder in circles of conflicting logic like a chicken without a head. In addition to the Wise Nod, I now acquired the Blank Stare into Space. Where do these great minds differ? At what point in this jungle of juxta-positions and jargon, this plethora of paradox and premiss, do you discern the definitive difference? So you begin to read books *about* the books, critical surveys, analytic assessments, flirting with Philosophy and Scientific Method, and slowly – very slowly – beginning – just beginning – to learn – *how* to learn.

Karl Popper, in his biography *Unended Quest*, writes of his 'dear omniscient master, Adalbert Posch . . . who taught me not only how very little I knew but also that any wisdom to which I might ever aspire could consist only in realizing more fully the infinity of my ignorance.'

That just about sums up my approach to learning and indeed to every one of my precious years at the School. I soaked up all I could manage of the great Karl Popper's course on Scientific Method! Every one of his classes was a cerebral shaft boring into that igneous rock of ignorance known to all tutors as the head of an undergraduate. Deductive or Inductive Method, the questionable value of Definition, Probability Theory – ideas to dazzle the mind, re-structure the brain. Science wasn't just Chemistry, Physics and Biology, it was a Method that applied to social as well as physical phenomena or anything else for that matter. It has stayed with me to this day, shaping everything I think or do or act. Sending me back, even now, to the methodological drawing-board in pursuit of a quirky little Enigma about not getting a fair slap on the back! The *Truth in Causality*! The Truth lying dormant below the surface, always there, simply waiting to be discovered! The *raison d'être* for this book! The only way for the Eternal Student! The Academic in the service of the Dramatic! Stanislavski would have gone for that.

But acting was oh, so far from my thoughts; I was all set for that Chair of Sociology. I could see myself up there on the podium on the first day of Michaelmas Term, dressed in a brown herring-bone suit, with perhaps the carnation in the button-hole, as befits a newly-appointed Assistant Lecturer in Sociology with three post-Shavian plays running in the West End. And pursued, even at that early stage, by the Enigma! What sort of praise would I have earned after my first lecture? Well, there's a sort of clue, if ever there was! But no hurry, it didn't quite work out that way.

3
The Smoking Concert

There's no question that Dr Popper's 'scientific method' did more to put my ideas into perspective than any other. But I began also to reassess my lecturers whom I had once found an infuriating waste of time. For I could dimly see that I was rising – with the inevitability of gradualness – to that primitive intellectual level that made their intellects intelligible to me. And I could dimly see that the more I journeyed in the mind, the less I would be able to communicate, eventually, with people who hadn't come along for the ride.

I dabbled in Aesthetics and read books on the History of Art. To tie this with my main studies, I read all I could on the Psychology of Laughter and made an analysis of newspaper cartoons to classify the type of joke and the form of the ludicrous involved. I actually began to send some of my cartoons to Fleet Street and was quite proud of my collection of Rejection Slips. For however much these efforts hovered between hobby and blocked vocation, the academic life was still my cherished goal, the university was my place. Still I dreamed that one day, from its Ivory Towers, I would shoot flaming barbs to burn down the Palisades of Myth and Prejudice that protect the Infidel – Reaction, and bar the Believer – Progress!

Ken Willy Watkins, Student Union demagogue – oh, what a speaker *he* was – started it. He suddenly decided that I should stand for Union Council. Me? Speak at Union meetings? Impossible! With Finals in 1950, not that far off? Impractical! Treating his sponsorship in the manner I thought it deserved, I drew a cartoon body with two necks, upon which I stuck two Polyphoto heads, and stuck this monstrosity on the board for council nominations. That was that! Next day, I was handed the Council Office key by Val Schur. I had been elected by 201 votes out of 230! And I am proud to say that in my period of office, as Chairman of the Refectory Committee (which led me, naturally enough to a study of the Manual of Nutrition and a book on Physiology), I did not speak once! Not, that is, until the last Union meeting of my Nodding office, where a wag stood up and asked me a long and complicated question about Refectory matters. I stood up and said, in a strong Welsh accent: 'I shouldn't be at all surprised, actually!'

But once elected, the chain reaction was set in motion. I moved up from *Beaver* office to the Union office, where the members spent their days playing liar dice and plotting lunatic coups. One of them was Allan Kingsbury, Entertainments Officer. And he plotted a coup in the Michaelmas Term of 1949, a coup which he called a 'Smoking Concert'. And because I drew funny cartoons, he assumed I could write funny material. It just so happened that from the age of 16, with a guitar bought for me by my mother, who encouraged everything I ever did, I had been composing awful tunes. And in cahoots with an old friend, Maurice Bentley, had moved on to writing parochial point numbers on the sexual proclivities of the Grange Park bourgeoisie. So I submitted a few ideas. Allan decided I should also perform them, and I cannot remember my reaction to that at all. Except perhaps, fear? But somehow it all went ahead. The smoking concert grew into a full scale revue, and I suggested it be called 'Place Pigalle', because that summer I had made my first trip to Paris, and had still to recover from the breathless excitement, the vibrant magic, of my introduction to Montmartre, Sacré Coeur and Pigalle! I had made a vow that one day I would grow a beard, go back to Montmartre, and paint – for the time being, I stayed clean-shaven and daubed the scenery for the show.

I was of course, quite mad! With nine months to go before Finals, I plunged impetuously into all the time-consuming, life-involving, wildly fascinating activities that go into putting on a show. John Hutchinson and Len Freedman were to do their brilliant double act at the piano; Al Bermel, then editor of *CMR*, was to write and perform; Cyril Wiseman, a law student who should have been a concert pianist, was to compose and accompany; and Bernard Levin (later, feared critic, controversial *Times* columnist, pundit and wit) was to impersonate Harold Laski and compère. I first met Levin one evening, as he was walking ahead of me to Holborn station. I caught up with him and said for no reason whatsoever: 'Did you know that Finsbury Park, spelt backwards, is Y-RUB-SNIF-KRAP?' He pointed out that KRAP-Y-RUB-SNIF might be more accurate, and I had found a fellow lunatic.

Oh, the days that followed! Casting, rehearsing, directing, rewriting, auditioning, re-casting, elation, depression, inspiration, exhaustion – all punctuated with interminable cups of coffee and inquests in Villiers Street. The Singing Chefs Sextet lost two, acquired Groucho Marx disguises, and became the four Grouchos. And driving us on, sustaining our flagging spirits, behind us all the way was the faith and energy of Allan Kingsbury, the finest natural producer I have ever met!

On November 15th, 1949, Place Pigalle went on. We under-rehearsed all day, adrenalin pumping from glands we didn't know we had, total chaos took on some semblance of shape, and I suddenly decided we needed a real horseshoe to set up a gag where we threw rubber ones (made Dad's workshop at

Elstree studios) at the audience. I left everything and every-one to hunt everywhere to find one – and I finally ran it to earth in an old forge housed in a seedy archway behind Kings Cross. Mortimer Wheeler never had it so good!

That night, the Old Theatre was packed with stamping, shouting students, thirsting for blood and targets for their wit! They greeted the overture with a barrage of huzzahs and toilet rolls! The predicted disaster was set before them! It was a huge, unbelievable, rip-roaring, runaway hit! Hutchinson and Freedman tore the place up, the Four Grouchos were a smash and the horseshoe gag was a socko boff. The cheers and laughter seemed to go on forever and probably did. And what was most important to me, my mother and sister and father were there and we all went home by tube, glowing over every blissful moment.

As for me, I had mumbled my way through rehearsals and nobody seemed to notice – we were, after all, bosom buddies in the same bumbling boat. But on the first night on the stage of the Old Theatre, something happened to me. I think I was born! Hearing that deep, booming, throaty, chesty sound of cackles and guffaws and shrieks – laughter! Who invented it I wonder? Who made me love it so much? What possessed me with the wild, mad courage to show off so publicly on stage when I was no better than a fawning, self-deprecating wimp? What madness got into me when I was standing behind the curtain listening to Bernard Levin introducing the next scene, and I stuck my head through the gap in the curtain and said in the voice of Jerry Colonna: 'The compere is of course, quite, quite mad!' Was it the rocking great belly laugh that followed and earned me more praise than anything else I did? I went on with the pusillanimous heart of a pigeon, heard the first roar of laughter for something *I* did, basked in the first cheer of approval for something *I* said, felt the first thudding heartbeat of success in a theatre full of scapegrace students who were *my* people, and came off with the heart of a lion!

I didn't sleep that night. I was floating a few feet above the bed on a cushion of warmth that flowed into my stomach and out of every nerve in my body. I had found the way to speak, to project, to be strong in public, to sustain a flow of words in public, to be a source of fun in public, and all by means of one simple device . . . I did it as someone else! And when that someone else was the greatest verbal wit of our time, and I could speak his words and use his voice and wear his clothes and lose myself beneath his Master's mask – in a word, when I could really feel that I *was* Groucho Marx – then all his power and glory passed to me. At second hand, perhaps! Derivative? Of course. But it was the only way I could have done it.

Not unusual, at this primitive stage, for the budding actor to imitate others, hide behind their pre-sold masks, then as confidence grows, to create his own persona. We could in fact say that the début at LSE was my moment of birth as a natural character actor, although that probably dates back to the age of two when at every family gathering I would lead all the other kids upstairs to raid the wardrobe, then back down in a Grand Parade of pint-sized prima donnas to the applause and clucks of proudly preening parents! By the age of six, I was doing impressions of everything and everybody – cars, guns, planes and Greta Garbo ('I vong to pee alone'), getting laughter, applause, personal praise! – no piffling little 'thank you's', by gosh, from this audience! – and all by means of that simple trick – doing it as someone else!

Well, isn't that what an actor does?

And where did it all come from?

Generally, from the Victorian Age of Parlour Poetry; the Day of the Amateur. The very same Reality Entertainment, which the TV companies are now trying to reinvent for us.

And specifically, from a father, Barney Moody, Professional Grocer, later Head of Department at ABC, Elstree, also Amateur Monologist, inspired in those days of Bransby

Williams and Sir Henry Irving to present parlour performances of *The Bells*, himself as the Mesmerist, his brother, Harry, as Matthias; *The Scene In Court*, a hilarious battery of neo-Dickensian characters; and *The Face On The Bar-room Floor*, a tragicomic monologue, one of many which he wrote out for me and which I am performing to this day, still using Dad's original, hand-written script. Not too late, I hope, to 'discover' and to admire a very funny man, and to thank him for passing it all on to me.

And on Kate's – my mother's – side, the music! Uncle Jack, literally bashing out *The Hungarian Rhapsody* on his fiddle in one minute flat (he gave me my first violin and took it back very quickly when I began to murder *The Bluebells of Scotland*); Uncle Benny, plonking away at the tunes of the day on a ukulele, surrounded by girls; Uncle Harry, pipe in mouth, wise-cracking non-stop with the best! Little wonder that a small boy of 6 or 7 would sit in wonder at these exciting evenings in the parlour Palladium, long before the days of radio and television turned the world into the Land of Couches and Potatoes.

So were laid the foundations of the actor and the mime. As a singer and dancer, I was totally untrained, but as an insatiable, three-times-a-week, seeing-it-through-twice movie-goer, I would come home imitating everything from Bing Crosby's *White Christmas* to Allan Jones's *The Donkey Serenade*, with patter songs and operatic arias on tap for the bathtime concerts. Similarly, my tribute to Fred Astaire was a piece of plywood in the kitchen where I would bash out a concatenation of clicks and thuds only equalled, in my opinion, by the Master himself, not to mention Léonide Massine's balletic leaps across the living room, sending the dog skittering under the table, and a peculiar corkscrew jump that I later learned to call an *entrechat*! My favourite step was a heel-slide-skip, best executed on perilously polished parquet floors, a step which I stole from Joan Davis, the acrobatic

American comedienne, star of the TV series *I Married Joan*. I discovered it was called a *pas de basque* many years later when I used it in *Oliver!*

All these steps were observed, collected and recycled. But there was one step that came from *me*; it was just a movement that I liked to do from childhood, my own thing. And when I finally saw it on the stage, I was astounded. 'But I've been doing that for years!' I muttered to myself when I saw Marcel Marceau doing his 'walking on the spot', followed by 'walking against the wind'. But even *he* couldn't wiggle his thumbs! Or his ears! Possibly his eyebrows? His nostrils? I did all that!

So was it not that all these childhood games and party pieces came together and found their spot, contributing to the euphoria I felt on stage that night at LSE, and was it not the fickle finger of fate that because of it I should dredge up an early childhood dream, long before I saw the Shavian light, to be a film star and go to Hollywood and marry Joe Pasternak's teenage discovery with the voice of an angel, Deanna Durbin?

Years later, when I actually got to Hollywood and, thanks to *Oliver!* and an Oscar nomination, was the blue-eyed boy of Columbia Pictures, I told the Studio publicist in all innocence about my worship from afar of the angelic Deanna! This eager beaver would very likely have had a meeting arranged and instant marriage announced in the *Hollywood Reporter*, unaware that some dreams are best left in the *Heavenly Herald Tribune*, but he discovered just in time that my sylph-like song-lark of yesteryear was now a buxom, happily married housewife, settled in mid-town America, with middle age and the middleweight spread that goes with it. Well, for me, that was it! When it's a fat lady that sings, the show is over, and in a way I felt I'd got my own back for her not having me when I was willing. Like Barkis in *David Copperfield*.

And, since we fatalists never question divine causality,

isn't it even more finger-fickle that I should get a Lower Second Hons, B Sc (Econ), yet be allowed to stay on for two more years, writing a PhD thesis, by that Guardian Angel and Registrar of Post-Graduate Students, Dr Anne Bohm, who was perfectly aware that my main thesis should not be *The Psycho-Sociological Aspects of Industrial Morale (sic!)* but *The Writing, Directing and Acting of Student Extravaganzas* with the inevitable metamorphosis to come of academic into actor. For that time to breathe, to think, to adjust to a seismic turning point in one's life, I am eternally indebted (as, I suspect, are many other graduate students) to that blessed lady. She worked her wonders at LSE well into her nineties, and even now, like Harold Laski, her great spirit keeps dreams alive.

4

Student Frolics

I was at LSE for something like five years, from 1948 to 1953. Physically, that is. Emotionally, my mind is still there, my heart and I remain forever, but we don't want to sound like something out of Franz Lehar. Two of those student years I would guess were showbiz contraband, smuggled in under the guise of a student society, serving the calling that had entranced me from the age of five, making people laugh! Why five? Alright, four, or better – when did I learn to 'walk against the wind' or tap-dance on plywood? It's what they call a 'calling'. It took so long, perhaps, because the war nudged me five years off course (or on?). LSE needed two more years than a degree. I was twenty nine before I turned professional because that was the time it needed. When you're at half a dozen cross-roads of choice, you need as long as it takes to find your path because that is what you will almost certainly buckle in and follow thereafter.

The student frolic *Place Pigalle* was my first full flexing of theatrical muscle. Like the first moon landing where space travel was suddenly no longer an illusion, so my childhood dream of starring at the London Palladium was suddenly (remote or not) a possibility. But it was still a dream, even though reality was opening doors all round, and I was alerted not only to the enormous fun of entertaining in public, but to the realisation that we didn't have to go begging for ways to do it. We wrote our own stuff and we put it on in our own Old Theatre for our own people! We didn't see any great drive to do more. It was fun! The amateur has always earned the respect of the English. In other words, if you don't ask for money, you are allowed to flex your muscles. So we did. We formed an unofficial Musical Comedy Society and flexed.

The following year, fellow student Al Bermel came up with the idea for a revue called *Freeziesta* and the rest of us chipped in with extra material. It wasn't very good, but it helped to elevate a one-off show into a tradition. So a year later, we did it again! Only this time, in discussions over coffee in the Refectory, we decided – all being ardent advocates of the Great American Musical – to go for a full-scale Great British Musical. We worked out a plot, writing about what we knew – the life of a student from Fresher to Finals – called it *Cap and Gown,* and Al and I divided the libretto between us. Cyril Wiseman wrote some excellent songs (he could have made lots of money as a composer, but opted for the law and probably made more). And I wrote a half dozen of the songs, because I'd been composing on the guitar since the age of 16, and, to my astonishment, they were all accepted. With *enthusiasm*! Doors that would have been shut down tight in the real world were opened wide and welcome in the good ship LSE. What do you call that? Over-indulgence in extramural activities? Wasting valuable study time? Or were they not in fact the seeds of the very encouragement to open up, to explore, to grow, to find the precious self that you came to University to nurture?

And here's a funny thing! The extramural activities were, in fact, incredibly intramural. The involvement in Musical Comedy needed music and it needed *comedy*. And that is precisely what this student was indulging in. I had discovered that every sociologist and every social philosopher seemed to have his own pet theory of laughter. Plato, Aristotle, Cicero, Quintilian, Bergson, Rousseau, Ben Jonson, Dryden, Descartes, Hobbes, Kant, Schopenhauer, all trotting out their 'intellectual' theories, 'degradation' theories, 'relief', liberty', and 'self-preservation' theories, essays, papers. The puzzlement is that with all the millions of words on philosophy that have been handed down, a subject as important as laughter has been relegated to little more than a footnote in social theory. But not for me. Laughter is as important to life and the survival of the species as food, drink, sex and a good lawyer. By 1949, my second year at LSE, 'The Social Psychology of Laughter' was my main peripheral study, my special hobby. And a delightful paradox! For my student hobby, writing comedy as a quasi-escape from study, had led me back to a totally committed study of laughter and the ludicrous, on the real-life boards of the living theatre! In fact, as I look back now, I can't understand why I didn't make 'laughter' the subject of my PhD thesis.

Anyway, I had by now sifted out from the mass of data a reasonable theory of laughter, based essentially on Talcott Parsons' *Structure of Social Action*, a thundering great tome from America that I had managed to read, annotate, and generally understand. The great man actually came to LSE to give a series of lectures. I sat through them all, took copious notes, went back over them and couldn't decipher a word. Anyway, I had taken Parsons' structural-functional theory, that is, where society is bound together by a set of ends or functions, criss-crossed by a lattice of social institutions, producing a well-integrated, socially cohesive society. Within these institutionalised patterns of behaviour, individuals are motivated by teleological (religious) or immanent (self-contained secular) ends which lead to habitual expectations. Any kind of deviation from these expectations produces a shock or surprise which manifests itself in laughter – or, if too extreme, tears. And such deviations may be contrived –

intensified – by odd behaviour or by clever writing – so that ludicrous moves or ludicrous lines get bigger laughs. Did you understand all that? Well, at least you can understand why it took me so long to adjust back to speaking normal English outside LSE!

My favourite example of contrived expectations is the *Four International Spies* number, which I wrote for a new musical, *Holiday Farm*, in the following Michaelmas Term, October 1951. A quartet of totally incompetent Russian spies enters and sings:

QUARTET	We're four international spies
ORSAKOV	I'm Orsakov!
BORSAKOV	I'm Borsakov!
KORSAKOV	I'm Korsakov!
SMITH (*a bespectacled Englishman with an adenoidal voice*)	
	I'm Smith!
QUARTET	We bump off inquisitive guys
ORSAKOV	I draw the gun!
BORSAKOV	I aim the gun!
KORSAKOV	I fire the gun!
SMITH	I mith!

And so it goes on, sets of four lines, three heavily-accented Russian voices setting up expectations for a fourth deep voice and getting the ludicrously strangulated bathos of dear old Smith!

Holiday Farm, a full-scale musical written and performed by LSE students with a small infusion of singing talent from the Guildhall School of Music, was really very successful. Nobody wanted to take it into town and we hardly expected it, but it started a buzz. There was a favourable review by Elizabeth Frank, showbiz journalist in the *News Chronicle*, and a lot of that contagious happiness that fills the air on amateur first nights however lousy the show. But for all that, it was the beginning of my early flirtation with show business. And Hymie Zahl called me in!

Hymie Zahl, the agency giant from Foster's Agency enshrined in the giant tower block overlooking Piccadilly Circus, had been in at one of the shows and had said that in a few years, Ron Moody would be leading the field! That was the first time I had had any Personal Praise from beyond the pale of our very student world and what with Elizabeth Frank and now this, I began to realise that 'things' were happening. So along I went to Piccadilly, still wearing my demob sports jacket – the only suit I still felt smart in – rising up in the lift through the dazzling adverts that ringed the Circus like spillage from Las Vegas, bringing a thrilling blush from the Sin City to the heart of London.

Hymie Zahl's office was huge with a spectacular view over Eros and Piccadilly, as expected, but the man was harder to find. He was very small behind his big desk and he peered over it through large, thick spectacles with eyes buzzing around like bees in a jam-pot. It was the Wizard of Oz!

'Frankie Howerd needs a new writer,' said the great Hymie of Oz 'Would you like to go along and see him?'

Frankie Howerd! One of England's top comedians and an exceedingly outlandish eccentric, *me* write for *him*? Why an amateur like me? I certainly liked to come up with the unexpected, I was a natural Edward de Bono lateral thinker, but did Frankie Howerd, with his own vividly established style, need my crazy student input? What the hell, crazy students, especially ones who are very broke, go along and find out how much is on offer, because respect is all very well for amateurs, but I – ex-serviceman's grant ended – was in dire need of dosh!

So a few days later, there I was, unemployed, at the fair old age of 25, with the heady scent of show business and a few bucks fast rising in my aquiline nostrils, appearing at the door of Frankie Howerd's lush pad in Holland Park.

I was ushered in by a very handsome, very young manservant who poured two drinks containing what appeared to be a thick white residue – certainly not sherbert – which I sniffed and sipped and left. I think I heard Frankie go 'Oooooh!'

Then I witnessed a moment of horror! The young man muttered something about expenses and Frankie reached into his trouser pocket and pulled out a bunch of crushed fivers! Crushed almost beyond recognition! Sacrilege! He shook a few of them loose for the young man to pick up, crunched the rest of the fortune into an even smaller screw of notes and thrust them unfeelingly back into the gaping maw of his trouser pocket. I swear I heard them rustle with fear! How could he do that to all that filthy lucre which I needed so much? Be *kind* to your dough, bread, mazuma, spondulics, moolah, boodle, gelt, call it what you like, but have some respect for the Englishman's dosh, described in better circles as his medium of exchange! I felt I was in a desert watching a sadist pour away my jug of iced lager.

We were sitting in Frankie's dimly-lit sanctum, melting by now into gathering dusk as Frankie began to talk about his comedic style and his backache and how it set him up in a hostile world, reflected in the deadpan stare of his po-faced female pianist, and how he had this debilitating backache, which was now the main part of the conversation because Frankie had somehow managed to slide from his chair onto the carpet, back first, giving out highly emotive 'Oooooohs' every time he made contact with or even reference to his aching back.

'You any good at massage?' he cooed at last.

I looked up from my notes on his technique and looked down at where his voice was coming from. 'No,' I said, wondering what one had to do with the other.

'Oooooh!' he said, and that was pretty well the end of that. It did not occur to me that my noncommital answer may have shot down any chance I might have had of fame and fortune and my first big break. That night I wrote out a comic monologue based on the clues gleaned from Frankie's backache – that is, his mutterings between 'Ooooohs' – typed it out and posted it and heard no more. Not even an 'Oooooh!'

The Ragged School in Clare Market, illustrated by me.

Interlude:

Memory Man, 1951

The young man was in his fourth year at LSE.

He was about 28. He had a slightly blue chin which encouraged him to shave a couple of times a week. His first tangle with celebrity had left him puzzled but wanting more. And oddly enough, the boys at the agency didn't seem too surprised at the Frankie episode or lose faith in Hymie's prediction. So the promising beginner was handed over to Junior, son of senior partner Gibbons, then introduced around the offices of the other agents, He chatted to the highly-civilised Max Kester, one of the nicest men he was likely to meet. Not too long after, he was called in to see Junior Gibbons.

'Do you have an act?' said Junior, fiddling importantly with papers.

Our hero mentioned a new act he was working on called *They All Wanna Play Hamlet.* Instant shake of head from worldly-wise Junior, steeped in the lore of the music hall for at least a week, signifying instant rejection of anything that sounded too clever, (including the Hamlet act which was eventually a huge hit).

'Well, there is *Frankie and Johnny,*' offered Hymie's Choice. 'I sing –'

'Go for it!' said Junior, 'I like it!'

'I sing the song on a guitar, and then do impressions –'

'Go for it!' said Junior, emphatic and final. 'I can get you a twelve-week variety tour, opening at the Granville, Walham Green, goodbye!' Arm flung wide, ending in handshake and even wider smile and the young man was out of the office, walking to the lift, beaming back at the faces beaming at him from the open doors of the other offices, wondering what he'd got himself into! Hey, Mum! I'm in show business! Yipes!

What kind of show business he was in he didn't realise until he turned up at the Granville, Walham Green, for the first day of rehearsal-cum-band call, and thought he was waved at by the star of the show, a rather well-worn middle-aged lady wearing a rather well-worn diaphanous dressing-gown out of which flopped too much of her rather well-worn skin. He was in a strip show! Junior Gibbons had done him proud! He was making his Variety début in the cheapest, dirtiest show in London!

The Musical Director was a fat little pigeon of a man, who seemed hardly capable of laughing or even pecking at whatever dots were put before him, so there was little reaction when the young man handed him a single printed sheet of *Frankie and Johnny*. The MD held it for a moment, turned it over, shook it, and looked at the vacant face before him. What he saw produced a shrug, a muttered '*Frankie and Johnny*, busk it,' a tap of knuckles on the piano lid and an opening chord. It went surprisingly well. The MD stopped playing after each verse for the insert of an impression, a gag, and a scribbled cue. Greta Garbo was Frankie, Bing Crosby was Johnny, Schnozzle Durante was the sherriff and Groucho Marx was the narrator, etc., etc.

But the first night was different. Quite a lot! It was as if he was suddenly sixteen again, never done it before, so what was he doing now, Postgraduate Student, billed number two in a tatty strip show in the heart of Fulham? The moment arrived. He stepped on! Deep dark silence. But by now he was not blinded by spots, he'd developed a tolerance at LSE and was able to see shadowy figures in plastic macs dotted all the way from front row to back. He was even able to see some faces – and chose to forget them. The curtains opened behind him revealing his table loaded with props, hook-on beards, stick-on tashes, hats, and, of course, a clothes-peg to clamp his nose for the rich nasal drawl of George Sanders. The joke was that the peg stuck and Sanders drawled: 'Looks like I'm stuck like this for the rest of the bloody evening.'

He stood there, 28 years old, a budding guitar virtuoso, about to stop the show! Something was telling him it was time to begin! It was a loud chord in E minor from the five piece band – on cue! – the fat little pigeon was not just a splatt in the eye. Our hero strummed his first progression and began to sing, in a rich, dark, Western accent (this he was good at, with his years of natural-born mimicry).

> *Frankie and Johnny were lovers*
> *Lordy, and how they could love*
> *Swore to be true to each other*
> *True as the stars above*
> *He was her man*
> *But she done him wrong!*

Music stops, in with first impression of Sherriff Groucho Marx (glasses and stick-on tash), 18 carat diamond cert of a belter at LSE . . . .

GROUCHO   What's all the commotion? No school tomorrow?

Nothing! He went on, patter, patter, patter . . . nothing, nothing, nothing . . . climbing back with some relief into the next verse . . . nothing! He plodded on, verse after verse, impression after impression.

Nothing! But at least his act wasn't dying. It was worse! It was running on and on, well over his allotted time.

Suddenly there was an ominous swish as the curtains closed behind him, cutting off access to his precious props. He was a 6-minute act, and he'd already done over 10 minutes. At least they had spared him the ancient practice of the pull-off hook! He stood there, looking at the bunched-up-at-the-front audience for some time, and he imagined they were looking at him but they made no sound, not even a derisive raspberry to cheer him off. They had paid for cheap seats and climbed over the seatbacks to get to the front, wolfish eyes glowing for the girls yet to strip in the semi-darkness.

He was affronted, muttered 'I 'aven't finished yet!' turned and went back through the curtain, reappeared with the clothes-peg to do his George Sanders – nothing! – and went on to the end.

There was still no applause. Nothing! Was he dreaming it? Maybe it was their dream? He turned to leave, couldn't find the exit till some sympathetic soul backstage jiggled the curtain through which he groped his way off in complete silence. He didn't remember any more. Maybe they dreamed each other?

The next night . . . again . . . nothing. The third night, Wednesday, a handful of LSE mates came in to support his amazing venture, failed or not. After all, what other PhD pundit could be seen to be researching his thesis in a tatty-nasty strip-show on the boards of a run-down theatre in Walham Green?

The idea that some of his people were in gave the lad new heart. There was actually mild applause on his entrance, and Groucho's first line got a laugh. No great success, no more than a mild beginning of sorts.

Until the fat little pigeon missed a cue.

The fat little pompous Musical Director screwed up!

He covered it quickly, went on, nobody noticed. Except that something stirred in our hero's breast, a sort of Spirit of Anarchy exploded therein, suddenly he didn't give a damn what these professionals thought, and anyway some of his people were out there! He walked over to the corner of the stage and looked down on the piano-conductor seated below.

'You missed a cue!' he said.

There was a big laugh!

'This is a great band,' he went on, 'They eat music, breathe music, they even sleep music! They just can't read music!'

POW! That was real laughter!

He'd actually got them!

For that one night, Moody had arrived. Helped on by his people, no doubt, but he knew now what it felt like to win over a zombie convention.

5

Love!

Unfortunately the triumph was short-lived! The fat little pigeon complained that the band had been held up to ridicule and I was ordered to stop. And in the following week at the Queen's, Poplar, simply running the act and not comprehending what I had discovered about the shock power of the ad lib at the Granville, the audience was ghastly, the backstage was ghastly, and I was not disappointed to be taken off the tour. Nor did I feel less than intense relief about the mouldering dressing-rooms and lust-jowled voyeurs I had escaped, let alone the slippery little tour manager who told Junior I had defaulted and would have to pay a fine. Junior told him that Harry Foster wouldn't like that and I was paid my full £6 and we heard no more. 'Nobody argues with Harry Foster,' grinned Junior. 'Face it! The biggest agent in Europe. They don't come any bigger!'

But I had to face the fact that I had no wish to visit the ugly underbelly of show business ever again. Danny Kaye at the London Palladium was still pure magic, Laurence Olivier at the Old Vic was still the stuff of masterpiece, but who needed the Granville, Walham Green, to aim for the bottom of the burlesque barrel!

It was a difficult time. I could now see myself at LSE, on stage at the Old Theatre, moving on mayhap to the world outside, winning mountains of Personal Praise as a comedian. But I could equally well see myself Personally Praised as a Junior Lecturer in Sociology if I ever really got down to work. So I did. With a supreme effort of will, I hammered out an outline: 'The Psycho-Sociological Aspects of Industrial Morale', and took it to Professor Ginsberg. To my joy, he was very interested in it, and in his infinite wisdom suggested I call it 'Industrial Morale'. I was back on the beam! But how *now* to decide? Things were hotting up on both sides! Would one settle for either on the toss of a coin, the spin of a wheel, was such a momentous decision, a life choice of such enormous consequence, to be left virtually in the lap of the gods?

I have long been convinced that the major religions, for all their ontological virtuosity and ethical magnificence, have lost out to the beguiling humour of the Roman gods. I am even now quite happy to accept these pagan supermen and women, playing their naughty little games with presumptuous mortals, indulging their capricious whims, and generally messing us about for the hell – or heaven – of it.

And they decided it was time for me to fall in love!

Head over heels – pierced by Cupid's dart, I could have danced all night, rotten with clichés and all of them apt – in love.

Her name was Isobel. She was a Social Science Fresher, and the most delicate creature of 19 I had ever met. I was 27, a Pre-Raphaelite in love, Degas at the ballet, Gene Kelly in Paris, Gauguin in Tahiti. I drifted – oh, incurable romantic – from bliss to despair, from happiness to misery, all turning on the capricious moods of a poppet that the Roman gods had thrown into the game because it looked like settling down into a boring and predictable academic career.

Who was there, I wonder, debating my fate on the topmost peak of Mount Olympus?

'I will not have it, Minerva!' Venus was angry. 'Industrial Morale, indeed! How boring!'

'Boring, my beautiful Golden Sister,' said Minerva, polishing Jupiter's breastplate at super speed. 'Boring as the bricks and straw that make a wall?'

'Walls make prisons, and don't you flash your eyes at me!'

'Peace, my Sisters!' Apollo smiled at the Maiden Goddesses. 'He may be building the wrong wall. Let us give the foundations one more really good shake and see if it holds.'

They showered him with kisses. 'Oh, Phoebus, from your throne of Truth, from your dwelling place at the heart of the World, you speak to men. What shake did you have in mind?'

Phoebus Apollo played on his golden lyre and outlined his plan, and the laughter of the gods echoed down from Mount Olympus and Bernard Levin stole Isobel.

Bernard Levin? My Bernard? My companion of so many hilarious japes and adventures, my witty, warm, and waggish friend, had we not worked in the Post Office that very Xmas to earn some bread, had we not spent the whole time playing chess behind the mail sacks and let the mail sort itself? My dear old Bernard? Could this be the spineless puppet that she preferred to me, Moody, kind, loving, sincere, honest, patho- logically possessive . . . could his be the limp dabs that now besmirched her gossamer fingers, on their shifty little walks behind my back in Lincoln's Inn, his the slack jaw that now sullied the sweetest lips in Christendom when I was safely out of sight? I decided to kill him.

It was the night of the Refectory Ball in June, and the clowns had evolved a slow motion boxing match inspired by, or rather, pinched from Chaplin in *City Lights*. It was a wow but I felt no joy. Isobel had just told me she was making a clean break for my sake. I cleaned off the clown make-up in the washroom with slow deliberation, walked like Pagliacci down the thirty flights of stairs to the main entrance and waited there with icy calm to bash his brains in.

'Do you think you have gone too far, dearest Apollo?' Minerva was worried. 'Do you wish to destroy the builder as well as the wall?'

Apollo stopped playing and laughed. 'Mercury, where is Pan?'

'In the woods, I suppose.'

'Well, tell him he has a little job to do – one of his clowns is losing his sense of humour.'

Oh, Levin, lustful, lecherous corrupter of Innocence, where art thou? Come forth from the darkness that I may slay thee with one mighty swing of my fist-bone! For now I shall verily drive thy buck teeth down thy gab-gifted throat!

But wait!

By the Great God Pan, what do I see?

I see thee slain! I see thee lying in the gutter with thy pointed little feet sticking up in the air. Oh, poor, pitiful creature, oh, sad thing I have done . . .

I spared him and went back upstairs.

But from that moment I wanted to show them! I wanted to show them who they had hurt, what a brilliant, talented fellow they had wronged! I wanted to be put on the stage and come back huge and famous with a big car, and show her what she had missed!

That was the time, the Michaelmas Term of 1951, that I wrote *Holiday Farm* with Al and Cyril. I directed it and cast it and made sure that certain people were not invited to be in it. I had the grim and petty (oh, so petty!) satisfaction (oh, so satisfying!) of seeing the outcast couple watching the extra gay and lively rehearsal from the darkness of the Old Theatre balcony; I had the wondrous satisfaction of directing the show to instant success and a rave notice from Elizabeth Frank in the *News Chronicle*; and in the following term I had the complete satisfaction of seeing Isobel and Bernard going their ways separately, their dastardly deed undone, their unlovely liaison lumbered. Cheap,but better than pistols at dawn. And so we became friends again – all of us – not so close perhaps, not so intimate, but good friends. For nobody could have helped it. The gods had played their tricks, the tricks had served their purpose, the die was cast, I was headed for show business.

And the metamorphosis of academic into actor came in the Michaelmas term of 1952. But whether or not it was those Roman gods again, having their fun, playing their tricks, the odds against it happening were formidable. There are seven twists to the tale. Let us trace each one in turn, just to see if some sneaky little Enigma pops out for serious scrutiny.

(1) Fellow student and co-writer Al Bermel spun the coin. Prolific and assiduous at all times, if you asked him for a sketch he'd deliver twenty pages by sundown. Little wonder he became Professor of Dramatic Criticism and Theatre History at City University, New York, has translated all the plays of Molière and Courteline and written a few tomes of his own including one masterwork called *Farce*. Anyway, back then in 1952, he decided that he wanted to do a new revue in the Michaelmas Term.

(2) '*No way*!' I said firmly. I had been at LSE for five years, I was 28 years of age, I had no prospect of any employment, my parents were beginning to wonder if LSE stood for Lifetime Scrounger Emeritus, and it was time to give up these happy little games, get in that bloody Library and consolidate my thesis.

(3) So I got in that bloody Library and consolidated an act called *They All Wanna Play Hamlet* in which Groucho Marx leered 'Ophelia! Get thee to a nunnery – and keep me a reservation!' and Jimmy 'Schnozzle' Durante destroyed the famous 'nose' speech from *Cyranner de Boigerac* which was nothing to do with *Hamlet*, but I was only a student, for heaven's sake! I also wrote a topical single, *Merry Christmas,*

Elsie, with a spiv Santa, decked out in sideboards, tash and drainpipes, singing:

> *'Ow about a little rubber cosh for Elsie?*
> *Or a dagger that won't slide into the handle?*

The revue was called *Rigor Mortis* and the students showed their appreciation with endless applause, loud cheers, and the mandatory toilet rolls streamering down from the gallery.

(4) A second night was mooted, nay, demanded! I was adamant. No more! Not a chance! I had serious, meaningful work to do in that bloody Library! Right? Alright, just one more night and that was it! Right? But I didn't want to do it!

(5) That was the one more night that I didn't want to do when Peter Myers and Ronnie Cass, the *enfants terribles* of intimate revue at the Irving Theatre off Leicester Square, came in to see the show, then backstage to see us.

'Moody, do you want to turn professional?' said Ronnie Cass, showing all the jagged edge of his irresistible Welsh charm, and Peter Myers stammered a lot and I couldn't hear too much because he spoke so quietly, but it began to dawn on me that these professionals were treating me as something more than a great big fish in the little sea of LSE, and as at least a tiny tiddler in the great big sea outside.

'I don't mind, really,' I said, rising to the peak of my ineptitude (Moody's Law), and wondering why I wasn't screaming out 'YES PLEASE! Oh, my God, gimme, gimme, GIMME, I do, I do, I DO!'

(6) I auditioned for the writers, Peter, Ronnie and Alec Grahame and the Manager, Freddy Piffard, at the New Lindsey, a tiny club theatre in Notting Hill. They were enthusiastic, but fully cast. So why audition me? Raising my hopes? Cruel! Five twists and turns of fate, now number six slaps me back into a jobless limbo. What was I to do this Xmas? I needed work, *money*, my Government Grant had finished

when I graduated two years ago! So how about a salesman at Harrods over the season? Or back to the Post Office, sorting the mail?

(7) Two weeks later, on December 7th, 1952, at 11 o'clock in the evening, deep down in the jobless depths of direst depression, I answered the phone. Peter Myers stammered into the earpiece. It *was* Peter Myers, wasn't it? Calling *me*? Yes, it was. To say a member of the cast had fallen out and did I want to join them? Did he say a member of the cast had fallen out and did I want to join them? Did he *say* that? Did *I* want to join them? DID I WANT TO JOIN THEM? There has to be a sub-text of mystical-hysterical laughter blended with fatalistic-crypto-orgasmic yearning beneath that line! (I need all those words to even begin to express how I felt!)

For goodness sakes, just look at the odds against! Given the marginally justified postgraduate years that Anne Bohm allowed me to have at LSE, we have (1) Al Bermel deciding out of the blue to do a new revue, (2) my refusal to appear in the show that I didn't *want* to do (3) but *did* to great success (4) with the second night that I adamantly *refused* to do but also *did* to great success (5) and this on the night that Cass and Myers happened to be in (6) leading to a professional audition where the show was fully cast (7) followed by the news that someone had dropped out at the last minute – well, it seems to me that a man is entitled to believe in a little more than a smidgeon of *destiny*! This is the fickle finger of fate out-fickled!

So, on 31st December 1952 and the seven twists of fate later, *Intimacy at Eight* opened at the Lindsey to unprecedented rave reviews, not to mention a leader article on the significance of intimate revue in the London *Times*, and I was off on the road to Olympus!

6

My First Theatrical Enigma

All the facts so far were checked against my 1948–52 diaries when I was writing a piece for Joan Abse's *My LSE*. Another example, incidentally, of my awful lack of judgement. That dear, gentle lady had to persist against all the odds and my evasive action in persuading me to write an account of my student years for the book she was compiling. But eventually, I did it. And found a second career as a writer . . . and surprise, surprise, ironically, it was Bernard Levin who had suggested to Joan that she should invite me to be in her book! Well, if you gotta do it, you gotta do it! So the diary entries are pretty well accurate and do not need further verification. But three days into *Intimacy at Eight*, my diary tells me I come face to face with my first theatrical Enigma! So soon? Is there a clue?

January 3rd, 1953. Feel wonderful and depressed by turns with each show. [So far I'd done three shows] *Ma, Pa and Cis come tonight! Good performance but Tony Edwards and the folks all say I look ill at ease. I don't feel it but I must try to find out what is wrong with me, if my 'feel' for the action doesn't reveal itself in my face. So we learn!*

January 4th. *Fenella* [Fielding] *comes to the matinee today and tells me I look scared. Other chaps in the cast have noticed that I am not always 'with them' . . .*

I didn't *feel* scared but I suppose working 'blind' on a professional stage in front of a critical professional audience – no chummy toilet rolls thrown here! – could have inspired a little subconscious terror? Plus the fact that my 'small fish' was now well out there in the 'big sea' of an enormous hit, and how did I ever, *ever* get to be *in* it? Add to that my desperate need for some kind of Personal Praise, from the family at least, to justify my very existence in the show – wait a minute, I mentioned Personal Praise! Can this little Enigma throw up the vital clue to the one that started it all? Alas, no. In the diary, the solution is far too deliciously dumb for that.

January 4th (continued). *Apparently I have been looking up at the spots instead of down at the audience. And of course I am still not at ease enough to ride a 'lost laugh'. I remedy the stare a little this evening. From now on, OK?*

Can you imagine? I had been too gauche to realise that I needed to adjust my performance to the size and shape of each theatre. I was used to playing to the house in the Old Theatre at LSE, where the stalls were just below stage level and the attention-grabbing yahoos in the balcony were about six feet above eye level. In the tiny, stalls-only New Lindsey, however, the entire audience was below eye-level, so with me Pavlov'd into playing my 'gallery' I'm surprised the Lindsey audience didn't sit with necks screwed round to see what I was looking up at! So Enigma solved, Personal Praise returns, no link to the dark mystery that launches us on our quest these fifty years later, by which time I know better than to look into spots!

All the same, Personal Praise is still the only viable

criterion of success. The enormous personal praise that I received as a student performer may be explained away as the audience's Parochial Pride in a fellow student, but the career that followed would suggest the debut of a rough, raw, untrained comedic spirit destined to expand and grow and, in so doing, come up against Enigmas that would inevitably lie beyond the growing boundaries of experience.

Where creative artists never cease to grow, so Enigmas never cease to appear and mystify. Seen or unseen, those serendipitous little sea-changes are lying in wait for us all the time!

Interlude:

Memory Man, 1952

1952. New Year's Eve. He was no longer a beginner, in fact he was eight days off his 29th birthday. And this night was the fabulous First Night of his first West End show, albeit an on-the-fringe intimate revue, *Intimacy at Eight* at The New Lindsey Theatre in Notting Hill Gate. And he had arrived at this point despite his terrible memory! He would dry at the drop of a syllable! But the audience rarely tumbled to it, because he had invented various devices to cover his flabby 'inward eye' (as William Wordsworth, poet, Romantic, and lakeside dweller, so neatly put it). Thus he would blame it on 'a dramatic pause' or 'a histrionic hiatus', sometimes looking accusingly at his fellow actor, as if that miscreant had forgotten the words!

Was there perhaps some perversity of nature that put him out of phase with his needs? If he had been a sound technician would he have been tone deaf? If he had been a lighting expert, would he have been colour-blind? Well, he was an actor and he had a lousy memory!

Knowing this, writers Myers and Cass, with all their rhyming skills and blazing wit and theatrical know-how, decided that his single, *Merry Xmas, Elsie*, developed by the 'boys' from an idea of his, needed a rewrite at the very last minute and delivered it to him, scrawled on a piece of paper, the very afternoon of the opening night.

With the memories still ripe in his consciousness of a forgotten *dunka-dunk* thirteen years before in a Victorian Church Hall, our hero gnawed at the piece of paper in the hope that the new words would somehow be cerebrally ingested, and fell to studying them with all the application he could summon up! It lay on his chest all through the Full Dress Rehearsal, distracted him from the laughter and applause that greeted every number on the First Night. He got through the main part of *Merry Xmas, Elsie* with singular success, leapt confidently into the final quatrain of altered words – and totally, utterly dried!

He stood there, looking at the newly invisible audience for some time and he imagined they were looking at him, but they made no sound, not even a derisive raspberry to cheer him on! Nothing! Was he dreaming it? Maybe it was *their* dream? He turned and walked off in complete silence, took the prompt copy of the script from the Stage Manager's desk, walked back on and read the last verse of *Merry Xmas, Elsie* with full Cockney impact! Still nothing! More like what one might call a state of shock. He returned the script to the corner and walked off again, in even completer silence. He didn't remember any more. Maybe they dreamed each other?

7

Professional Anarchist

I spent six fun-packed, high-pressured years from '53 to '59 With Messrs Peter Myers, Alec Grahame, Ronnie Cass, John Pritchett and David Climie (all bona-fide Trevor Griffiths-type writers of *true* jokes) at the Lindsey, the Criterion, the Apollo and the Strand Theatres, learning my trade in the essentially anarchic world of intimate revue and cabaret.

It all started with *Intimacy at Eight* in my own very special club theatre at Notting Hill, and to my great good fortune it was directed with great flair and devilish wit by John Regan, who could see I was a greenhorn and got me to hang around to see how the production worked. He was a crazy Irishman from Limerick, whose wild cackle and blazing blue eyes concealed a prankish perception of his fellow man and a Rabelaisian perception of his fellow woman. Shall I ever forget his cry, 'There's a titter running through the audience', as he 'tittered' round the stalls, bouncing imaginary boobs? The stalls were empty, but he would have 'tittered' if they'd been full! And enjoyed it more!

Sadly, although he was full of inventive ideas and hilarious touches, John never directed the West End editions of the revues, possibly because he was, dare we say, charmingly unpredictable and not always totally all there . . . physically, that is. Between shows, and maybe during them, it appears he returned home to run his Dancing Academy in Limerick, though I suspect his true home was Lady Gregory's Garden in Coole Park, County Clare, where the Little People gathered to welcome back their fellow leprechaun.

The West End revues were staged with all the form and dynamics of a full-length ballet by puckish jet-setter Michael Charnley, classical dancer and choreographer, notorious for his first-night greeting to the cast – an agonizing neck massage equivalent to Edward Scissorhands plunging his steel points into your trapezius. Since Michael's gift for comic business ended there, Ronnie Stevens, brilliantly precise in performance, was chosen to apply the same skill to blocking the sketches. The small orchestra was led by the most intuitive accompanist and piano conductor in the business, Ronald Cass. (We generally kept to the three variations, Ron, Ronnie and Ronald, but if somebody shouted 'Ron!' three heads would still turn.) Prolific writer Peter Myers, with his unerring choice of the right spot for a spot, laid out the running order – the true secret of intimate revue. And only then, with this solid, iron-cast structure driving the revue forward with relentless pace and variety, were we, the laughter-makers, given space to learn our lines and moves and, with full approval of the authors, to feel free – oh, the joy of creative freedom! – to create our own characters, build the business, slap on the shtuck, punch in the topical lines (usually served up from the orchestra pit by avid news reader, Cass) and get that audience rocking with deep-down-in-the-belly-fit-to-bust-and-right-on-target-laughter! And yet we still stayed within the bounds of convention; no hint yet of the pop, pot and pornography that was to erupt in the Haight-Ashbury district of San Francisco in the '50s, and morally turn the Western World on its ear with the permissive society.

Even so, there were lessons to be learnt from allowing a cast so much licence: that freedom implies responsibility; that you can dribble the ball and take the kick, but you learn how to pass; that you share your shots; that you keep the ball moving; and the goals belong to the team! With the goal posts right out there in the audience!

Now wait, wait, *wait* a minute! Have we not just read a florid description of what has to be the most perfect, smooth-running, self-regulating theatrical Ensemble ever? Do we not have here the veritable apotheosis of Creative Fellowship, the eulogizing of a pure and selfless denial of personal ambition in the service of the Comedic Art? Comedians actually *sharing* a laugh? *Feeding* each other? Why then, we have here the Ensemble of Ensembles! But! If this is so, how do we reconcile these saccharine sentiments with the bitter diatribe against ensemble playing? As well as the stirrings of Truth, do we have here, perhaps, the bitter-sweet taste of Paradox?

An ensemble that is most certainly *not* an ensemble is most certainly a paradox. In that over-fond summing up of six years of revue, I may have given an overview impression of an ensemble, but there were four revues and each one was different and Creative Fellowship was hardly the term I would apply to any of them!

For example, in my first professional show, *Intimacy at Eight*, far from being welcomed as part of an ensemble of equals, the cast treated me generally as an outsider, a talented but untrained amateur from some dubious left-wing institution off the Strand. Regan was always an enormous help, Cass was always rude, but since he was only rude to people he liked that didn't count. We stayed close friends for over 50 years and he got ruder all the time. Dear old Ronnie. I think that the exquisite Eunice Grayson, whom my mother named 'Euston Station', kept away because she knew I was madly in love with her and who needs it? Of the rest, Joan Sims and

Charles Ross were charming. Joan was a funny lady, oh what a funny lady! She had the knack of making straight lines funny. She could get a laugh out of a word, a comma, a look! And she had a heart to match. Charles Ross accepted me at once, but then he wasn't just an actor, he was a businessman. He was a theatre manager. He put on plays, opened elegant restaurants, simply liked people. The rest were distant. If I spoke to them, they might answer. If I walked up to a group of them, I had the uneasy feeling that they would disperse, and they did. I seemed to have a natural knack for pooping parties. This was nothing like the egalitarian ensemble of *Comedians*, where we all stayed in line and forfeited Personal Praise, this was personal rejection. But was there enough mystery in this for even a faint Enigma? I *felt* like an outsider. I *behaved* like an outsider. I *was* an outsider. I had been at LSE for five years, I could only talk fluently in Talcott Parsons' structural-functional sociological jargon, otherwise I was half-way incoherent. As a PhD student I would go back to LSE from time to time to find a familiar face in the Refectory and have a coffee and an in-house chin-wag. I was still doing it a year later . . .

> ***March 26th, 1954.*** *Meet Charles Stewart at LSE, nattering to Mike Curtis. Have tea in the Refectory – almost as we used to a few years ago. But how different the circumstances are now. How wonderful to have no more of those dreadful day-dreams and empty aspirations and futile heartaches that kept me from achieving fulfilment – but how awful to think of the narrow margin by which I almost missed the big opportunity. I still have a long way to go – but it's great to have started.*

As an actor, I was an anarchist on stage with a monumental inferiority complex off, and painfully, *painfully* shy. No, definitely no clue-bearing Enigma here, but perhaps a tasty little Paradox! Because it all worked out for the best. Instead of dealing a calamitous blow to my self-esteem, the inimical ambience had the effect of strengthening my resolve and building up the bloody-minded reserves that you need to survive fifty-odd years in a tough profession. I vowed, quite simply: 'I'll show you bastards!' and worked harder!

And there was more grist to the Will! When the revue transferred to the Hippodrome as *High Spirits*, and was re-cast with revue-meisters Cyril Ritchard and Ian Carmichael leading the company, Charles Ross and I were left out. Again, not as calamitous as it might seem, for, as one of the original members of the hit show, still running at the New Lindsey, the take-over cast actually treated me with *respect*! As one of *them*! By not transferring me with *High Spirits*, which oddly enough didn't run that long, they had unwittingly blessed me with the finest gift a beginner could desire – belonging! I was suddenly a 'pro', a Professional Comedian, running with this pack at least! My confidence burgeoned, I got more laughs, I knew they were mine and how I got them, my feet were at last standing firm on the professional stage, and I never lacked for Personal Praise, so I had to be doing something right. Maybe the solution to the Oxford Enigma would be found precisely here, in something that I was doing right and not wrong? Was it in being more than just one of the team? In *Comedians*, I had no friends, only fellow workers. At the Lindsey, I was beginning to make friends in an atmosphere of mutual respect, friends like Jimmy Thompson and Thelma Ruby, to supplement the ever-loving mob at the School. And though under it all I still hissed 'I'll show you bastards!' and worked harder than ever, things were changing and new best friends were hovering in the wings.

More Intimacy at Eight opened at the New Lindsey exactly one year after the first revue. It enjoyed a successful week at Brighton Theatre Royal, then on April 29th, 1954, transferred to the Criterion Theatre in Piccadilly Circus as *Intimacy at 8.30* and brought with it the incomparable Joan Heal, one of the best-known names of musical theatre in the '50s.

Joan was about the same age as I was, but had started much earlier in the business and was a highly-trained revue and musical comedy artiste. A graduate of the ultra-sophisticated Globe Revues, where she met her husband, Jeremy Hawk, she had that wonderful special quality called class, and with it went taste, chic and glamour, which in the old days of Hollywood used to be called 'it'. She looked at this evidently talented, belly-laugh-raising, clodpoll youth making his debut in the West End, with pipe thrust in mouth and hair hacked off at the neck, still wearing, would you believe it, his demob sports jacket and other shapeless sacks, and decided to do something about it.

She ordered the immaculate Digby Wolfe, who shared my dressing-room, to introduce me to his tailor, Mr Clenshaw of Airey and Wheeler in Piccadilly, and his barber, David of Piccadilly, who in turn introduced me to his bank manager at the Piccadilly branch of Barclays, so there I was, *au fait* with the West End, all toffed up like an actor and a long way from Turnpike Lane. Where I still lived. And where my mother was quite ecstatic to see that her son was finally wearing a nice suit. Not to mention a natty tie and light brown, soft leather chukkahs.

Also, I had somehow during the first year in the business managed to get into the clutches of an Australian singing teacher named Holmes, who was of the opinion that high notes could be best achieved by constricting the throat. Fortunately he decided to go back to Australia, where he no doubt opened a school for lost voices and so saved me from a similar fate. Joan put me in touch immediately with her own singing teacher, Ernst Urbach, a handsomely-built Viennese who was once an acclaimed opera singer and now specialised in infusing operatic size and timbre into the resonant cavities of straight actors. He decided I was a tenor and in no time at all had me reaching top C's and singing *In Fernem Land* from *Lohengrin* and *Nessun Dorma* from *The World Cup*. When asked why she helped so much, Joan said she loved talent. Where else, I ask you, could you hope to find a better compliment?

From that time on, I grafted! There is no other word for the hard, relentless drive to succeed that pushes everything else into second place. Tap-dancing lessons with Buddy Bradley, modern dance at the Dance Centre, singing lessons with Ernst, here was growth time for the LSE clown, a wild, eccentric, natural mimic developing into a professional anarchist, a sing-in-the-bath crooner opening up into a trained tenor, a plywood-bashing amateur hoofing it into a 'lovely mover!' Here was the time for doing new things, breaking new ground, borrowing fewer masks and building more creative and original ones of my own! For example, in *For Amusement Only* at the Apollo, three years later in 1956, apart from *Rita*, a biblical scena at the end of Act One, where I impersonated everyone from Groucho and Durante to Bing Crosby, Alastair Sim and Robertson Hare, I was not only developing original characters but, ever the perfectionist, adding lines, touches and nuances at every performance until each comic persona was filled out, polished and only then fixed.

Interlude:

Memory Man, 1957

1957. Our hero, now a man of 31, had become a valued member of the revue team, entrusted with complex comic numbers that needed an inventive mind, and a flair for comic business called *schtuck*. Spelt *shtick*, or *stück*, it was American/German qua Yiddish for a 'bit' or 'piece' of physical clowning.

For example, in a loose bit of burlesque – very simply, laughter for laughter's sake – he beefed up a musical scena by wearing a sort of crocheted cloche hat 'borrowed' from his mother's wardrobe (oh, the props he plundered from dear old Mum!) with a pair of ear flaps sewn on and tied by string to a long-stemmed Alpine pipe held in the mouth! (All the best clowns make their own props.) When I took the pipe from my mouth and lowered it, the ear flaps went up. Pipe back in mouth, ear flaps dropped. And all done with a heavy German accent. 'Why? What's the razz, the satirical point?' they asked him. 'Shut up and laugh!' he replied.

This all took place in *For Amusement Only*, the most successful of the revues which ran two years at the Apollo Theatre and was the only one written entirely by Peter Myers (what falling-out was behind that?), with music by Ronnie Cass and John Pritchett. And if there was burlesque a-plenty, there was satire a-plenty. There was a devastating send-up of

Liberace by Jimmy Thompson at the grand piano with candelabra, and lawyers licking their lips for a court case. The murderous mock of amateur musicals by the whole company, which included Hugh Paddick, Louie Ramsey (Inspector Wexford's wife on and off TV), and the operatic lip-trembler Thelma Ruby. When Thelma used to deputise for Joan Sims on Sunday nights, I used to shout out, 'Sunday Night is Ruby Night!'

And there was *Davy Crockett*! Disney had just begun to make films with humans instead of cartoons, and *King of the Wild Frontier* with Fess Parker was a big hit. How could Peter resist a number about the fortune made by Walt Disney commercialising that heroic figure from the old West? And how could Ronnie Cass resist adapting the hit tune so that nobody had to pay a fortune for using the original melody?

Davy Crockett was one of Peter Myers' best singles – how that man could write under pressure! – but it went into the show on the last matinee at Brighton because he wanted to try it out before the West End opening at the Apollo. Given such short notice, it was an impossible feat to learn and perform it unless, of course, you had an artist with an incredible fast-soak, photographic memory, and the ability to perform the number pretty well off the cuff. And there was only one man whom they could depend on to deliver the goods by sundown! The Memory Man himself – the legendary amateur from the London School of Economics – Ron Moody!

He went to work at once. Knowing that he would be lucky to learn half the punctuation marks by the next day, he asked for a sheet music copy of the song, with a picture of Fess Parker on the cover and all the words printed inside. He attached the music to Crockett's carbine, photo facing outwards, words facing inwards, so he could literally read it on stage! It was an advance on *Merry Xmas, Elsie* five years earlier . . . and it worked! As for setting the number with no rehearsal time, our hero dressed in traditional garb with frontier rifle, powder horn and flat Tennessee accent, totally deadpan, throwing away every line, ad-libbing gags to fill gaps ('This ain't no powder horn – I'm deef too!'), moving one step sideways at the end of each verse, and timing the finish to move the last step sideways off the stage.

'I've turned in my grave in Tennessee
I'm just as livid as I can be, since I discovered my
*   destiny*
Was to make a fortune for Walt Disney;
Davy, Davy Crockett, King Technicolour drear!
Walt's makin' a fortune selling to brats
His Davy Crockett outfits, that's, there's a lot of fur on a
*   lot of hats*
Which means a lot of folks have lost a lot of cats!

8

Enter the
Clown

Diary, June 5th, 1956. [Day of the First Night at the Apollo Theatre] *Peter wants me to leave out my Davy Crockett ad libs. Ronnie persuades him to leave them in. All through this bloody show Peter has tried to leave out my own pet ideas, the stupid, pot-bellied oaf* [my diary is full of splenetic insults, but no harm in it, just writing things I don't have the nerve to say, everybody comes in for their fair share]. *Have flowers sent to all the girls and buy some leather cuff-links for Ronnie Cass and Peter who however stupid, made all this possible.*

So much for fond memories of the 'full approval of the authors . . . punch in the topical lines'! Ensemble? Pah! In addition, I wasn't too happy to be given my single at number two in the cold, cold minutes of the First Act, but as Peter stammered: 'Y-y-yes, but think what it does for the show.' Well, there's an ensemble line if ever there was! But I had to admit it was true. Getting big laughs so early in the show generates a challenge and a law – save your best for the end, but put your second best up front.

The best that was saved for the end was, of course, the

legendary *Vagabond Student*, the classic last word on amateur theatricals. I have never heard such laughter in a theatre, before or since, nor have I ever read anything so unfunny as the original script. Franzl, the hero of this pastiche of a Lehar operetta, was loaded with long speeches made up of blank dotted lines, signifying, I assumed, silence. With, I assumed, laughter expected on the responses to the silence. But an inaudible hero will get one laugh on the first silent speech, then nothing. It was necessary to ring the changes! So I went through the entire script, writing in not merely the missing lines but lines that would offer a whole series of comedic audible variations in the strangled, nasal, glottal sounds that such a man would make. Peter allowed all this without a mutter, after all I wasn't changing his lines only his dots. And when he heard the never-ending tumult of laughter, he did at last relax and yield to us the comedic autonomy that I so fondly remember. Added to which, I was making his impossible hero possible. But who or where was such a character?

By sheer luck – oh, the joys of Serendipity! – I was taken by a dear friend, Maurice Bentley, to see a Viennese operetta presented by the staff of his local library. And the hero of the piece, a youth who should be preserved in aspic in the Theatre Museum was that character! St. Vitus never came into it – this fellow twitched, shook, gyrated and bounced, with his stupid great supine hand thrust out front all the time waving to and fro like a drunken waiter trying to balance a tray of rampant eels! His head had a life of its own, rotating from side to side as if it was scanning the audience for help! And when he *sang*! Yi! The strangled, nasal, glottal sound started somewhere at the back of his throat, seemingly aimed at the young lady who was 'singing' with him, but one could not tell because his eyes never stopped rotating, mostly rolling up and back into their sockets as if he had been merci-fully rendered blind to save seeing the faces of the audience! I sat there in silent hysterics, the whole image imprinted indelibly in my memory. By sheer chance, I had found my character! And the world of literature had found its definitive, unqualified, unconditional, categorical, Thesaurus-bending exemplar of Serendipity!

The result was a cruelly biting and relentless satire on amateur theatricals that had only one saving grace for the victims – if they had come to see it, none of the blithering orks (who had actually received a standing ovation, would you believe it, from their carers!) would have recognised themselves and been offended. As Jonathan Swift put it: 'Satire is a sort of glass wherein beholders do generally discover everybody's face but their own.' Perhaps therein is the strength and the weakness of satire – that it may delineate its target in painfully meticulous detail, but it cannot *change* the object of its ridicule because all is vanity and nobody ever sees folly in themselves. And if they did, would they want or be able to change? (Trevor Griffiths, please note.)

As I wrote earlier, *The Vagabond Student* was notorious for sending the ladies out of the theatre with mascara streaming down their cheeks and sometimes the premature evacuation of other essential bodily fluids! Backstage they would come, still mopping their eyes, full of fulsome Personal Praise that had the peculiar effect of making me feel not flattered, not egotistical, but simply normal. It was as if the huge, rolling belly-laughs and the nightly storm of applause and the backstage praise were needed to maintain in me a perfectly ordinary sense of self. With them, I was complete. Without them, I felt the cold hand of failure rummaging around my viscera – what an awful thought, but it sums up the way I felt at Exeter and Oxford in *Comedians*, just in case you had forgotten why I am writing this book. And why you are about to enjoy a lolloping great Enigma that happened during the two-year run of *For Amusement Only*, one that baffled us for months and was finally solved in the simplest of ways by the least likely of observers.

Quite simply, though it became the most successful of all
the revues, *For Amusement Only* was born in chaos. In spite
of that earlier description, 'the most perfect, smooth-running,
self-regulating theatrical ensemble ever', I have to confess that
those fair-spoken words came straight from the heart and onto
the paper as I remembered them. For that memory was warm
and happy and complete! I loved *everybody*! They were
halcyon days! And it hardly seems fair to subject them to the
gamma rays of Truth, by opening the pages of the dreaded
Diary. But the Truth is exactly what we must have if we are to
show how a mix of incongruous personalities can meld
together to produce, not the dream-team Ensemble, but a huge
success followed by a truly depressing Enigma! And it all
began in rehearsals . . .

> *April 6th, 1956. Up early and off to the Piccadilly
> Theatre for first call at 10.30. It is music mostly and Peter
> gives out material.* [I never found out why, but Peter was
> doing this one on his own. Cass and Pritchett were still
> on music, but there was no Alec Grahame or David
> Climie around to battle his mulish streak, or contain his
> renowned constipation complex, hoarding every
> precious word he wrote and refusing to change a comma.
> The trick here was never ask, just change it, do it and
> pretend you learnt it wrong. But what had we let our-
> selves in for?] *Thelma* [Ruby] *isn't coming back from
> holiday until Monday . . . Louie* [Ramsay] *has an eye
> affliction and won't join us until Southsea . . . Jimmy*
> [Thompson] *has an impacted wisdom tooth and isn't
> coming until tomorrow . . .*

And what of Peter's legendary skill with the running order?

> *April 12th. Have our first run-through this afternoon at
> the Inns of Court and it isn't too bad. But some of the*

numbers will have to go. Actually we are rehearsing about 35 [enough for a five hour show!] so the chopping down process will have to begin as soon as the shape of the show emerges. And who knows what that will be?

And what of our director and classical ballet genius, Michael Charnley, who let it be said, was a great companion, warm, talented, creative and never there?

April 14th. Michael is away in Monte Carlo directing his ballet in honour of the Grace Kelly wedding.

April 19th. Have futile day waiting for Michael to come back from Monte Carlo – there are still some tricky numbers to be set, let alone polished and we have about 10 days to go.

The following general entry seems to sum up the mood:

April 22nd. If ever I put on my own show I shall never allow such low morale to develop in my company as has been the case in this one. What weak, ineffective leadership . . . there is a battle of egos going on with a vengeance between the so-called principals [for material] and I alone of them have accepted what I have been given without a murmur.

I never argued about material. I think I looked for the challenge on the page, not the milk-fed certainty of a show-stopping lyric. Whatever the material, accept it, explore it, add timing and stück and make it work. I did this with 90% of my material which may well be why the hard-pressed writers promoted me in each succeeding show until finally I was billed above the title in *For Adults Only*.

For Amusement Only opened at the King's Theatre,

Southsea. I don't know if it was the audience or us, but the First Act died. Then Jimmy got huge applause as Liberace, the show picked up from there and the diary reports:

> *April 30th.* *The Vagabond Student is the big hit and my character goes down beautifully! What a relief that those rehearsal laughs weren't phoney.*

Hardly the promise of a move to town, but there was enough in that first night to give us all the faith to slog on, particularly Peter Myers who was single-handedly cutting, re-setting, re-writing and rehearsing new numbers which he always wrote best under pressure. So it went on, all through the rest of the tour, from Streatham Hill, where '*Pam Manson* [actress and theatrical agent] *and her friends are in and tear it to pieces*', Cambridge, where we had a '*hysterical under-graduate reception*', to Brighton Theatre Royal, traditionally cold and sticky, the better to prepare us for a warmer lift into the West End and a triumphant first night at the Apollo Theatre on Shaftesbury Avenue '*with loud cheers and 12 curtains!*'!

Having thus seen a near-flop transformed by sheer, hard, daily, nightly grind and determination into a long-running hit, I thereafter looked upon the first night of every tour that followed, and even of every first night in the West End that followed, as the beginning of hard work, the continuation of re-writing and rehearsal, with the advantage of nightly audiences to test out the show. And perhaps, because *For Amusement Only* was one man's victory (with a little help from his friends), born in chaos, and surviving against all odds, it was inevitable that a sense of anarchy never left it, its drive came from within rather than from a strong directorial hand above, and any Enigma that happened along would be that much harder to solve. And it was!

The Vagabond Student, the flagship scena, began to

misfire! The funniest piece of block comedy in the revue, probably in *all* the revues, possibly in any revue ever, was losing its laughs! And a lost laugh is quite the most maddening thing to get back. It just seems to be gone forever. And the bunch of fading laughs that make up a dying scena is an Enigma almost beyond solution. The creative team, born in anarchy and given its specialties and its perspectives, didn't know what to do. Michael Charnley had never been involved in the comedy direction, he focused on the dancing and the rhythm and pace of the whole show. Ronnie Stevens as sketch director might have helped, even Hugh Paddick, Thelma Ruby, Jimmy Thompson, Ron Moody – we all might have seen what was wrong but we were on stage, doing it. We needed a specialist, an expert, somebody out front to tell us.

The peak of the scena was Franzl's inaudible, rabble-rousing speech to the peasants. To make it work, I had actually written a speech, insisting, in rather gruesome detail, that the most awful physical indignities be heaped on the person of Hugh Paddick's villain! I confess that I offered a stream of disgraceful scatological suggestions (for which I apologise), wilfully intended to corpse the cast lined up each side of Franzl, yet to remain out of earshot of the audience who, seeing the casts' faces, was dying to know what I was saying, although some who came backstage afterwards insisted they had heard every word (for which I *really* apologise). Naughty Moody!

Barely six weeks after the Apollo opening, the strain was beginning to tell.

July 17th. *The initial zest is wearing off now that all the creative impulse has crystallised into set patterns of business.*

Time to open it up again! As a result, the 'silent' speech got longer and longer, I had to virtually improvise at every performance, not merely a different flow of words to enliven the cast, but pregnant silences of varying lengths just to experiment and see how long they would hold, and bizarre gestures such as a sinister chopping motion of the hand signifying the sad fate of the villain's masculine pride. It was the most exhilarating exercise in creative comedy that I have ever been privileged to develop, sustaining the comedic variations all through and building to the near-cabaret spot, the stand-up bit, the 'silent speech', at the end. And even here, amidst this runaway personal success, or probably because of it, I was confronted with a mini-Enigma, a problem oddly enough on the Ethics of Laughter-Making.

> *July 18th. I am rather worried about the Vagabond Student because the final oration, which I so enjoyed, has now become an argument which Ronnie [Stevens] has worked into it – I think it spoils the mood and damps it down.*

Well, here was a puzzle. I had strict principles about laughter-making:
Never kill another man's laugh.
Be just as happy feeding a laugh as getting it.
Aim to increase the risibility of a scene, never decrease it.
Get the laugh, then make it real.
As for competition, no cheap tricks, win only by being better and sticking to principles.
So what do I do here? Ronnie Stevens is quite legitimately increasing the risibility of the *Vagabond*, I am feeding him and we all welcome extra laughs, but he is thereby intruding into my special moment. Since he now intrudes, I have lost control over the carefully orchestrated pauses, I am no longer leading the action in this area. But it is against my principles to kill the laughs from his very funny interruptions.
What do I do?
Fortunately, others saw my dilemma and acted.

July 25th. Peter Myers, now back with some new numbers, calls us on stage for notes between shows and he tells Ronnie to cut out the crosstalk in the 'Student'.

Win by sticking to principles? Bravo! Conscience clear and back to normal? Excellent! And of course, no rancour towards Ronnie, an excellent fellow laughter-maker! Oh, and there's a little more to the diary entry: '*Good. That will teach him not to try and cash in on my gag, the bastard!*'

This incident is not a digression, it is, in fact, a direct clue to the solution of the *Vagabond* Enigma where the lost laughter was still a source of great concern. Let us return to it with a look at the diary, which shows that the problem was with us some seven months after the opening . . .

November 13th. Another call this evening to run through the Vagabond Student for a check on all the rough edges. It is pretty well set anyway and the check should have come months ago before the odd business intruded and established itself.

December 15th. . . . the houses are fine and I have recovered the laughs in the long speech – I tend to let it go from time to time. Still it has lasted for eight months so I can't argue.

Recover the laughs, lose the laughs, so it went on, good houses, bad houses, great nights, poor nights, business intruded, business removed, we were used to the stuff of long runs. But in the late spring of 1957, around the end of the first year, we were suddenly losing those wonderful long, rolling laughs with the ever-present, helpless feeling that they would never return. We were deeply puzzled, eventually alarmed. Was it the timing? Had we lost our characters? Had we lost control? Was the audience demographic changing? Was the coach trade missing the point? Was it somebody coughing? – perhaps, but not on every line! Well, here was an Enigma qualitatively different from Oxford: we were getting the Personal Praise for the show, but somehow people didn't seem to think we were funny any more! So what, oh, *what* were we doing wrong?

I mentioned earlier that it was finally solved in the simplest of ways by the least likely of observers. The show had been running for nearly a year and the cast had settled into an ant-run of visits between dressing-rooms, fitting in with times onstage and times offstage, something that a few years before at LSE I would have called 'institutionalised patterns of behaviour'. Now it was my time to visit Jimmy Thompson's room a floor above, and his wife Nina was there. They had married during the run, with the whole cast present, and we had continued the celebrations into the Apollo, done a good semi-sober show sprinkled with quips aimed at the happy couple, and finished up in the '*Student*' by throwing confetti over Jimmy! Enormous one-off fun, since Peter Dalby, the Company Manager, had announced the wedding up front and the audience were in on the whole thing!

So now Nina was nearly always there, keeping Jimmy company in his dressing-room, probably even dressing him but I never asked about that. Anyway, she was there. And James and I were off again about the boring old Enigma, what was wrong with *Vagabond*? Character? Timing? The threshold of laughter? The weather? And Nina cut through all the theatrical claptrap and said, 'I sat out front the other day and it seemed to me you all think you're very funny.'

You all think you're very funny!

I looked at Jimmy and Jimmy looked at me, and I forced myself to recall that I had only been a professional for a couple of years or so and had no right to patronise presumptuous amateurs or snigger at their bovine opinions especially when those opinions were absolutely, Lord Help

Us, Gawd Luvva Duck, bloody-well right!

Lots of things happen on a long run, and the worst of them is to believe your publicity, remember only your good notices, listen to your Mother who never thinks you're on stage long enough and that everybody is waiting till you come back on, and then, drunk on laughter, believe you are a very funny person! Instantly, your funny character goes out of the window, you, yes *you*, climb back in, intruding your silly little smug conceited self into your performance, and proceed to bury everything that made you funny in the first place!

June 24th, 1957. Call at the Apollo to check over the Vagabond which has deteriorated grotesquely. Lots of points cleared up and I am happy about my bits. But Cass, the chief offender doesn't come to rehearsal. Bloody fool! This evening the 'Student' is reborn again. What a relief!

Cass (Ronald) the chief offender? Bloody fool? How? Quite simply, he had always been part of the onstage show, always more than just Musical Director Supreme sitting aloof in the pit, uncanny in his sensing of a point number and timing of a funny lyric, solid as a rock on tempos and pace. He also liked to *laugh*! He liked all of us to know he was there for us, out front, our best audience, laughing at all our funny stuff however many times he had seen it, so we would never feel alone with a sticky audience. Ronnie always insisted that he wasn't laughing for us but for *himself* because the show was so brilliantly funny, happening afresh every night! Whichever way, he was wonderful for the company morale, no 'chief offender' here. But perhaps when the well-meaning pixie in the pit laughed at everyone's funny little bits – a short step to everyone feeling funny – and knowing it – well, instead of being true to their characters, they were all thinking 'Everyone is looking at *me* and, *oh*, what a funny person *I* am!'

All at once, we have no focus, no centre of attention, no hero – alright, say the awful word – no star performance holding it together. We have happy anarchy! 'You all think you're very funny!' A strong, comedically informed directorial hand might have prevented it, kept it structured, contained the egos, but failing that we were lucky to have sweet Nina to put her finger right on it, and teach us all a lesson.

So easy to see now where Ronnie Stevens' intrusion into the 'silent speech' was a clue. Everybody – not just him but *everybody* – wanted to get into the act! Who can blame them for wanting to be part of the intoxicating hilarity of the *Vagabond* – which of course they already were! It had always been – what am I saying? – a comedic Ensemble in intent! But never in fact!

Unfortunately, none of the Enigmas so far has given us a clue to solving the original Oxford Enigma where it seems 'Personal Praise is still the only viable criterion of success'. *For Amusement Only* was a hit show where, be it a good or bad night, there was no shortage of Personal Praise, even when there was a shortage of laughs. Two very different mysteries, it seems. But are they? Can there not still be something deeper, a logical link, perhaps even a Law, that explains all these various Enigmas under one overall Principle?

For Adults Only, the last of the three Myers/Cass revues, opened at the Strand Theatre on Monday, 5th May, 1958 with a cast that included Louie Ramsey, Hugh Paddick and Miriam Karlin. If ever a revue was the antithesis of a luvvie Ensemble, this was it. If *Amusement* was born in chaos, *Adults* was born in hate! Strong words for two little shows, but Peter, now back with Alec Grahame, had decided on two sets of alternating compères – two dear Old Ladies and two sweet Young Yuppies. During rehearsals the Old Ladies won by a knitting needle and the Young Yuppies were down-sized! But not fired! Ouch!

May 5th, 1958. The show is in a ghastly shape partly because Louie [Ramsay] *and Richard* [Waring] *are now free to do things in the show since their links didn't work – so there are too many people trying to do too few things and there are three people above the title* [Miriam Karlin, Hugh Paddick and Ron Moody] *who ought to be properly featured but aren't. Stupidity from the top downwards but mostly due to* [wait for it!] *Peter Myers. The mime is very rough but I can only begin to polish that now that we are touring and I can have the actual set and props to work with.*

A full account of this revue would fairly compare with a Shakespearian tragedy or a television soap, all you could ever want of back-biting, back-stabbing, jealousy, intrigue, ambition, treachery, everything short of murder and even that if looks could kill! Or get a laugh! I will say no more, to protect the guilty. Except that Peter Myers again saved the day (with a little help from his friends), providing new material that pacified the warring factions, and never never never giving up! The man was a marvel and the show ran nine months at the Saville. So much for *Adults*. There were no Enigmas or Serendipities worthy of note, but by sheer chance I am happy to announce that we do have a truly momentous Paradox to save the day! It is no more than a small phrase from the diary note above, '*the mime is very rough*' but it is probably more important than all the diary notes put together. Paraphrasing a speech from King Henry IV, Part I, I misquote: 'Out of this nettle *Adults*, we pluck this flower, *Pierrot*.'

Pierrot at the Airport was the name of the mime that I was allowed to create and include in *Adults* – in fact I was contracted to write two singles but I held the second in reserve – I would still do whatever Peter gave me and try to make it work, but no harm in a little personal insurance. And speaking of insurance, you may ask why I would choose to take such a risk as writing and appearing in a classical mime inspired by Jean-Louis Barrault playing Jean-Gaspard Deburau in *Les Enfants du Paradis*, which was without question my most favourite film of all time? And why I, for some time, had been thinking of myself as a Clown rather than a comedian, and then again, by Clown, not a red-nosed prat-faller in a circus but a tragi-comic Actor in a Theatre? Dreaming perhaps of becoming some kind of protean minimalist, seeking to move his audience from laughter to tears on the turn of a phrase or the flick of a finger?

What then was the Paradox? Why, simply that in *Adults*, the last and the least memorable of the Myers/Cass revues in which I appeared, I should make an unexpected impact in a wordless mime, a theatrical form quite untypical of the verbal wit associated with intimate revue, but which proved for me a giant step towards later growth. From the crude burlesque of student revue, to the enriched mixture of professional satire, to the turning point of mime which, seen by Robert Lewis, the New York Method director, led to new depths of characterisation in *Candide*! What's next, I wonder?

This brings up a whole kettle of inspirational *poissons*, dating back to the first time I saw Marcel Marceau in the West End in November 1957, and had the uncanny feeling of deja vu which was not that uncanny since I had deja vu'd the film of *Les Enfants du Paradis*. I had also in 1957 been reading Robert Payne's masterpiece *The Great Charlie*, which had an enormous influence on my work and writing and my understanding of Clowns, although the diary reminds me:

November 7th, 1957. It is infuriating at times because he [Robert Payne] *tries to read mystical intentions into purely impulsive comic business, but there are some useful tips to be picked up . . .*

In this book – essential reading for any comedy actor or writer – despite his insistence that Charlie was the Great God Pan, Payne traces the formative influences in the life and work of Chaplin from primitive laughter-makers through the Greek Zanni, the Roman Atellane farces and the commedia dell'arte to Deburau in France and Grimaldi in England, and this is where my favourite female clown, Vivienne Martin, makes her appearance. She was actually with me in *For Amusement Only* for the whole two-year run, an experience and a companionship which I can only describe as 'heavenly' because that sounds a little nicer than 'unearthly'.

Vivienne was in her early twenties when she took a steam package from New Zealand to England, where she took a steam train from London to Oldham, where she steamed into the local rep and demanded a job and got it. (In fact she 'hitched' to Oldham, but 'steam' is a nicer word to play with.)

She turned up at the Piccadilly Theatre for the first day of rehearsal and I began to write things in my diary, pretty well as I remember them now.

April 13th, 1956. Have wonderful afternoon rehearsing 'Clacton' with Vivienne – a real nice girl this one.

A few weeks later, on train to Southsea for the first week, I wrote:

April 29th. I spend most of the journey with Viv who is such a nice lassie compared with the other complex girls in the last show.
May 5th. [Early hours] *I'd almost forgotten what a contented mood one can derive from the right sort of female companion. We wander along the moonlit beach – gee, ain't this the romantic! . . .*

And she ran into the sea! Cried out to the pitch darkness and the ocean's mystery! A wild child, back-dreaming to her native New Zealand. I should have seen the light then. Meanwhile, I clung to the promenade, hoping I wouldn't have to call out the coast guard! Hardly surprising that in no time at all I was writing:

July 31st. Managed to pull Viv out of that silly mood last night but it looks as if we are doomed to unending conflict, each going off at the other. Might be better to finish it.

August 3rd. Go to the Jack of Clubs with Viv . . . suggest we leave pretty soon after the cabaret in case she does anything embarrassing, and I am not at all surprised when she jumps into a taxi and leaves me standing in Oxford Street. Old stuff! But I am surprised to hear her running back after me, terribly sorry for her silly mood . . .

The 'real *nice* girl', so much nicer than 'the other *complex* girls', the 'right sort' to lull me into 'a *contented* mood', turned out to be the most highly-strung, unpredictable, serenity-busting kook I had ever met in my life. Every evening, going into the theatre, I never knew what mood she would be in. Or for how long. And if she did something that put me, quite reasonably, into a sulky mood, she would have the audacity to throw a sulky mood right back at me, and she had absolutely *no right* to do that when it was *my* turn to sulk! Alright, so I had a tendency in my youth to cut people off, isolate them into a cocoon of silence if they offended my puritanical standards; not speak to them for days – a jolly habit I inherited from my mother – but, dammit, Vivienne had no right to do it *back* to me! *No woman had ever done it back to me before!*

So there we were, deeply attracted to each other, deeply resentful of each other, unable to escape from each other because we were trapped with each other in the two year run of a smash-hit show. Well, anyone with any sense, you scoff benignly, could still have cut it off and looked elsewhere. Didn't I *say* that! Didn't I *try* that? Didn't we break it all off regularly once a month and twice on festivals, then, feeling as free as the birds, fall back in deeper than ever before!

Whatever we did, however we tried, nothing worked because, as we discovered later, we were in the power of yet another perverse and prankish Paradox! The tempestuous relationship that forced us apart all through the run and had us bouncing backwards and forwards, in the best of times and the worst of times, was the same paradoxically powerful bond that held us together.

We were both Clowns! On journeys, conjoined, to lands of magic and adventure! Kindred spirits, with an instinct for the things we both had to do, the things that were right for each other, above all, those things where we could help each other to grow and give each other the courage to do it! And that I needed more than anyone! I hadn't done too badly so far but that was mostly due to Peter Myers and Ronnie Cass, offers from a sprinkling of agents and writers, and my ability to write my own material for cabaret. Nothing more, except perhaps a blind drive to success, a deep-rooted ambition to write the Great British Musical, a comparable ambition to re-create the Golden Age of Comedy on film, all centred on a bizarre talent, a love of shtuck and an atavistic funny-bone. But I still think it was a miracle that I made anything at all, because, let's face it, one of the more attractive of the personality traits sprinkled so generously through this text was a total inability to make up my mind! If I tossed a coin to help me decide, I would do it again, then do the best of three until it came up half way to the way I really deep down wanted it. I think.

Vivienne told me what to do without hesitation! And she was instantly right. How do you break a bond like that? Especially since this bond was never more powerful than in the eventual realisation that we were both Clowns, Tragi-Comic Actors, walking the well-trodden, Pagliacci-belted, Bel-Canto'd tight-rope between laughter and tears. Vivienne's inspiration was Giulietta Masina in *La Strada*, mine was Chaplin, the Marx Brothers, Keaton, Durante, and everybody else from the Golden Age.

But that moment of realisation, though it was underlying all the work we had so far done, did not bubble to the surface until '57. I had been so utterly fascinated, researching the history of the Clown in Robert Payne's book, that I bought a copy for Vivienne. It had the same instant effect on her. These were the great times – after the show – between tiffs – sitting for hours in a coffee shop over a *cafe au lait* and a rum baba – when a paperback book, like an *Alice Through The Looking Glass*, provided a shimmering portal through which we passed into the magical, mischievous world of Clowning. 'Mischief' became the keynote, the shibboleth of the new Clown team. Vivienne even made me a mosaic of semi-precious stones with the word 'Mischief' cemented in reverse to keep its secret. I have had it from that day on my dressing-room table, wherever I have been playing in the world, to remind me who I am.

So here we were with *For Adults Only*, and my decision to experiment with my single spot by presenting a white-faced, classical French mime. Vivienne was not in the show – she was away in the Middle East, working for Combined Services Entertainment, entertaining the troops and developing in line with her newly-defined vocation as clown. But we were still in touch. And any cringing, pusillanimous suggestion from me that I do the original Guitar Act with words met with stronger words and *no* doubts that I should go with the mime! Wordless!

Anyway, I had to have the stomach to go for this chancey little jaunt pretty much on my own. Well, not exactly 'chancey' – I had learnt in cabaret never to do an entirely new act. Always begin with a piece of tested material to check the audience strength, and after the risky new piece, which may fail, have the solid ground of a tested spot to fall back on. That way you never lose the audience.

In *Pierrot at the Airport*, I simply adapted my *Guitar Act* from cabaret, six minutes of tested transmogrification with words and music, ringing the changes on national ways of using the guitar! Pierrot, a porter at the airport, pushing a guitar case on a small trolley, takes out the guitar, explores it, and as he hears the flight departure announcements over the Tannoy ('voiced' by Freddie Jaeger) finds that it becomes a finger-trapping flamenco guitar in Spain, a capsizing gondola pole in Venice, a straight cricket bat in England, and a shapely dance partner to a Strauss waltz in Austria, crumbling along with Pierrot's romantic dream into the realisation that he is dancing with nothing more than a wooden guitar and that he is, as he trundles his trolley away, as always, alone.

So I knew there were laughs built in – I just didn't know if they would happen without words. Well, they did – every single one. Plus new rich chortles triggered by looks, gestures and the wonderful sense of control that comes from the commanding silence. After a few weeks, I forgot that words had ever been there! And oddly enough, for someone who had always gone for the big gesture, I never mugged or went over the top. The ludicrous action came from the heart and a wonderful feeling of stillness and control. Truly, a turning point in a career!

The moment of Truth, however, our physical initiation into the Great White Faces, or as Payne might have put it, the Mystical Brotherhood of 'The Great God Pan', did not happen until the last great Chelsea Arts Ball which took place at the Royal Albert Hall on 31st December, 1958. It was no big deal.

My dentist had tickets, and Viv and I decided to go as Clowns – Circus Clowns. With check suits and big boots. You know – some do it with red noses.

> *December 30th, 1958. Into town to pay Martin for the Chelsea Arts Ball and order some costumes from Aubrey Samuels. Tom* [the wardobe-master, who could pull your size from his racks with half a glance] *picks out a lovely selection of clown outfits so that Viv and I can have some choice and I will collect them tomorrow. Also buy a book on circus clowns in Foyles – an American book showing make-up methods and established acts of their best known clowns. But how different they are from the French tradition with their bouncing slapstick and prop business, clutter with excessive frills and fripperies, too sentimental perhaps, and too much slap on the face. The more I do my mime, the more I love the plain white face, simple and clean cut. I have a lot more to do on this yet.*

Oh, how exciting was that Chelsea Arts Ball! Something special was beginning, and the choosing of the costume and the tinkering with the make-up set the seal on it. Washed to bits and near-hanging in strips, an old tee-shirt went on him first, a pretty vest on her, clearing the decks for the moisturizer, the skin-soft base, the Clown white, the black liner. Neither spoke, the only sounds were the grunts of surprise, the tiny cackles of delight in their discovery of the persona and the finding of the face. She produced a pretty little mask with cupid's bow twinkling beneath small pink nose, smiling like a contented kitten who had just seen off a saucer of warm milk, and was ready to spread love throughout the world!

He became a blank, near-to-nothing, watcher-in-the-mist, an opaque blueprint of a man looking down his prod-nose at the world, his head turning slowly to record all that passed before his wide-open, black-ringed eyes!

They arrived at the Albert Hall with minutes to spare, he drove into the forecourt to park, a policeman tells him to move on, he argues with the policeman, tells him they're going to miss the bloody New Year ('Are you swearing at me, sir?'), looks like they'll greet it in a cell, she tells him not to be rude, the rozzer doesn't arrest him, lets them park, they get into the Albert Hall just in time to greet the New Year amidst the crazy fancy dress and colour! What a wonderful time with all the revellers and the exhibition floats – and then the bathos of the smoke bomb which some idiot lets off, sealing the fate of the greatest show on earth – it is never put on again! And that is when our two clowns discover themselves and who they really are!

She was the catalyst for all human life, constant in her mischief and spreading it around; he was mankind's witness, seeing deep into the hearts of men and understanding! She ran around and around and around the milling crowd, joining up unattached boys and girls with irresistible authority and insisting that they dance; he lifted not a finger but left them alone. Nobody joined him!

And so they passed that magic night, always together in spirit, always aware of each other, yet millions of eons apart in the cavorting mêlée that filled the Albert Hall with colour and life and (I swear it showed in every way) with love!

For it was indeed an evening of innocence and love, an evening of evenings when clowns were born, when night ran into day. But that was how we lived! Because there was much, much more to this era. Half the performers in the West End went on after their shows to work the clubs. Twenty pounds a week was hardly enough for anyone (save an ex-student who had run out of funds) but another £20 was *money*! So, with the unconscionable innocence or, dare one say, retarded awareness of a Candide reborn, I had plunged straight into the late-night cabarets of some of the toughest clubs in London. The *Hamlet* act which I had written as a student, fitted perfectly into the milieu of outrageous drunks, chinless aristos, warm-hearted call-girls, cold-eyed villains, and the corps of night-club hostesses locked away upstairs in the 'cage' till feeding time for the sucker tourists. Champagne at £70 a bottle (1950s prices) popping everywhere, wurst and eggs for breakfast, money and drink flowing like water and an old LSE boy King of the Cabaret! I ad-libbed outrageously, loved it when the hecklers were on form, and willingly sacrificed the structure of the act (yet never lost the spine of it) for the joyous anarchy of an unscripted interchange, a battle of wits with the show-offs and the loud-mouths and who cared who won!

The point I am trying to make with this potted biography of my early days is that an unschooled innocent, a tongue-tied academic fresh out of college, with an all-consuming love for his audience and a single-minded, overwhelming desire for nothing more than to render them helpless with laughter, found his true comedic, freedom-loving soul in the *nostalgie de la boue* of the West End netherworld. And not always hiding behind other people's masks!

Interlude:

Memory Man, 1959

1959. *The Night That Bernstein Came.*

He was about 35, he had been in the 'business' for about six thrilling years, grown to thespian manhood with a new-found cloak of confidence that, believe it or not, descended upon him the day he passed his driving test! *Ecce homo*, the diffident amateur now blossomed into professional all-rounder, about to make his giant step from the protean versatility of revue to the drama-driven foothills of musical comedy. Sounding good? And yet it is interesting to note that so far, despite the exciting introduction of six years in revue, his world was strangely lacking in the one element associated above all with his beloved 'Show Business'. Glamour! The stuff that stirs the masses, hits the headlines, sells magazines in international airports, and for those who think of nothing else, pulls the birds! He had none of this, give or take the occasional backstage visit of a captive star when he was introduced, tongue-tied, to the likes of: Groucho Marx, the incomparable, who actually spoke to him and had a picture taken with him, to be printed soon after in the *Picturegoer*; Jack Benny, the master, who poked his head round the dressing-room door and, as he lived and breathed, seemed to be saying nice things about him; Tyrone Power, who took a shine to Thelma Ruby and took her to dinner a few times; and of course, Charles Laughton, who came back to meet the company and told Ronnie Cass that Ron Moody 'had the timing of genius!'

But this was before *Candide*.

Imagine what happened when our hero was cast by the great New York Method Director, Robert Lewis, in his first musical which was also the first English production of the great Leonard Bernstein's classical pastiche *Candide*, adapted by the great Lillian Hellman from the 100-page tale by the great François-Marie Arouet, otherwise known as the great Voltaire, with choreography by the great Jack Cole, sets and costumes by the great Osbert Lancaster and production stills by the great Tony Armstrong-Jones. How do you like them apples? Great enough? How do you like the idea, in your first major musical, of being encircled by some pretty impressive Brits and the greats of the Broadway Theatre, the cream of the dramatic and choreographic talent from what was, in 1959, the Master Race of Musicals?

So here we have our hero cast as the Governor of Buenos Aires, known to his enemies as Don Fernando de Ibarra y Figueroa y Mascareñas y Lampourdos y Souza (his friends called him 'Y' – pronounced 'eee'), a sleazy seigneur who wined and dined his droit and was consigned in turn to sing a solo, a quartet, an ensemble and a Bflat. That's a high note. The young man's singing teacher, Ernst Urbach, was confident he could do it. Sometimes in class, he got him up to top C sharp but didn't tell him he was doing it. Now, as Governor, he would have to sing a Bflat every performance and *know* he was doing it! And he did it! And knew it! Boooon Voyage! There it goes! Top of the World, Ma! Bingo! Bel Canto! Let It All Hang Out! Oh, it's all going to go so well! On this, the night that Bernstein came! Nervous? Me? Yahahahaha!

Wait! Huzzah! It is bruited abroad that the great man is not only coming, he is coming round after the show! *Coming round*! One of the great geniuses, one of the all-round great composers of the American Musical Theatre *coming round* to see the cast! To see little ol' *us*! Yipes! Encomium upon encomium! Kudos upon kudos! Paean upon paean! Give that man a cigar! Who cares if he doesn't smoke? This is a night that will go down in history! This is something to tell our grandchildren! Let's face it, this will have to be the performance of our *lives*!

Bravado? Nonsense! Our hero is a seasoned performer, who cares nothing that somewhere down in the stalls, he can feel the eyes of a genius seeing him, the ears of a maestro hearing him, the laughs are rolling nicely, they reach *Bon Voyage* and our brave young man begins to sing the Governor's tenor solo with chorus, and cracks on the B flat!

May 7, 1959. At show tonight hear that Bernstein is in . . .
I don't do good show

Bernstein didn't come round to see me afterwards. I think he saw everybody else. I also think I broke his heart.

May 8th, 1959. Useful singing lesson – Ernst says Bernstein was astonished to hear my voice after I had done such good comedy – the combination I suppose surprised him. Still, it's nice to know.

From that day, on Ernst's advice, I hit *Bon Voyage* an octave below, did an octave-jump to the Bflat above – *Bo-hon*! – and brought the ship safely ashore every time.

With Mater.

With Dad. Not too late, I hope, to 'discover' a very funny man and thank him for passing it all on to me.

'What, no ice creams?' The Moodys on Brighton beach. From left to right: Cis, Mum, Ron and Dad.

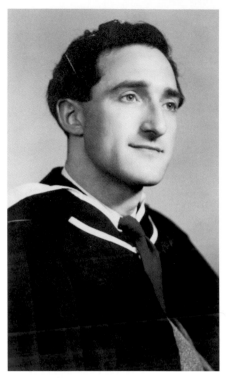

My son the Graduate.

My first words to Bernard Levin, 'Did you know that Finsbury Park spelt backwards is Y-RUB-SNIF-KRAP?'

'The teacher lives on', illustrated by me for the *Clare Market Review*.

The talent! Left to right: Al Bermel, Cyril Wiseman and Yours Truly.

'Two year run, one ear done in!' The Vagabond Student in *For Amusement Only* with Thelma Ruby.

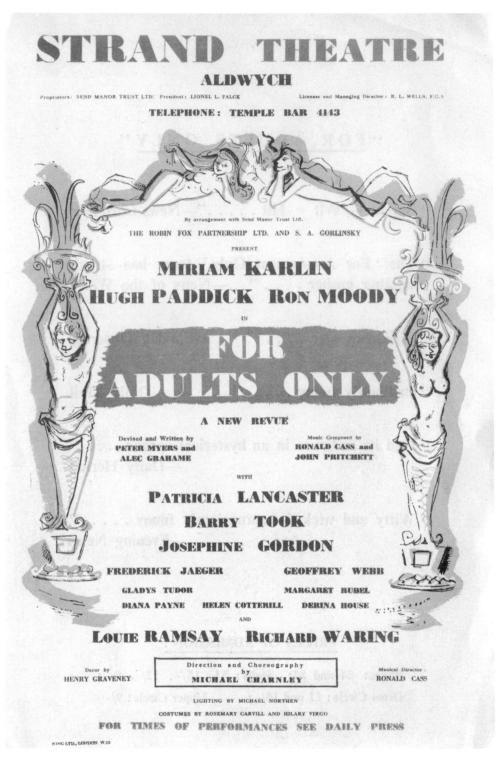

STRAND THEATRE
ALDWYCH

Proprietors: SEND MANOR TRUST LTD: President: LIONEL L. FALCK   Licensee and Managing Director: R. L. WELLS, F.C.A

TELEPHONE: TEMPLE BAR 4143

By arrangement with Send Manor Trust Ltd.

THE ROBIN FOX PARTNERSHIP LTD. AND S. A. GORLINSKY

PRESENT

MIRIAM KARLIN
HUGH PADDICK RON MOODY

IN

FOR ADULTS ONLY

A NEW REVUE

Devised and Written by
PETER MYERS and
ALEC GRAHAME

Music Composed by
RONALD CASS and
JOHN PRITCHETT

WITH

PATRICIA LANCASTER
BARRY TOOK
JOSEPHINE GORDON

FREDERICK JAEGER   **GEOFFREY WEBB**

GLADYS TUDOR   MARGARET RUBEL

DIANA PAYNE   HELEN COTTERILL   DERINA HOUSE

AND

LOUIE RAMSAY   RICHARD WARING

Decor by
HENRY GRAVENEY

Direction and Choreography
by
MICHAEL CHARNLEY

Musical Director:
RONALD CASS

LIGHTING BY MICHAEL NORTHEN

COSTUMES BY ROSEMARY CARVILL AND HILARY VIRGO

FOR TIMES OF PERFORMANCES SEE DAILY PRESS

KING LTD., LONDON W.12

The first time my name appeared above the title with Hugh Paddick, one of the funniest men I'd ever seen and the marvellous Miriam Karlin, the astonishing mistress of a thousand accents.

Pierrot at the airport.

Return of the Vagabond Student Curly with Pat Lancaster.

As Hamlet in cabaret.
MOODY: 'To be or not to – er – um – er –'
BAND: 'BE!'

The Governor

Over powdered look round the chin.

Very cerné under the eyes.

THE GOVERNOR OF BUENOS AYRES, DON FERNANDO D'IBARAA
Y FIGUEORA Y MASCARENAS Y LAMPOURDOS Y SOUZA
"CANDIDE", 1959. MAKE UP DESIGN BY OSBERT LANCASTER

The Governor by Osbert Lancaster from *Candide*.

The Governor from *Candide*, photographed by Tony Armstrong-Jones. A present I've always cherished!

MOODY: 'Nice suit, Groucho!'
GROUCHO: 'I wish I could say the same for you.'

Moody recording his flamenco special . . .
'I tell you the story now
Of a most ambitious cow
Who wanted to fight in the
Bullring in Seville.'

Ron Moody and Vivienne Martin at the last Chelsea Arts Ball.

Ron and Viv.

Fagin with the first Oliver, Keith Hamshere.

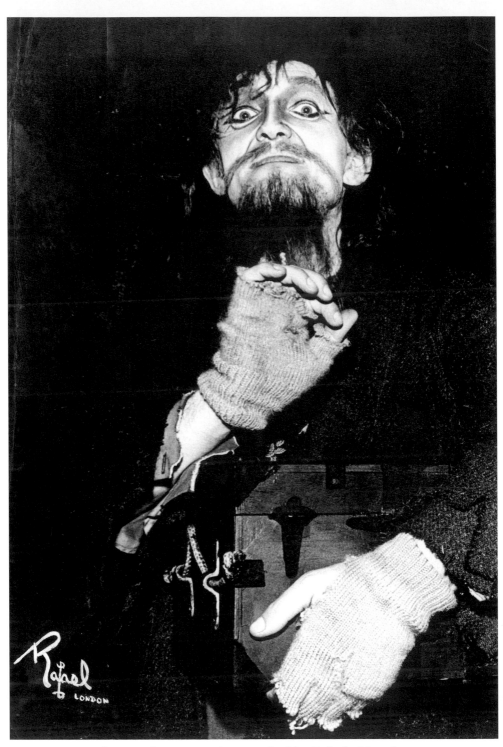

The very first Fagin photographed by Rafael of London.

MOODY: 'Ere, Lionel, Grub up!'
BART: 'Please Sir, I want some more?'

Georgia Brown (Nancy) and her Dickensian denizens in full flow.

Fifty years on . . . and still at it!
All the way to the Gods!

9

The Ahk-Tor!

But back to the beginning of it all.

The first read-through at the Saville Theatre, 10 o'clock, Monday 23rd February, 1959, was more terrifying, more humiliating, more downright, damnably degrading than being knighted in the nude. I hadn't realised it was such a *big show*. I was used to a revue cast of eight, maybe ten. Here we had forty! A pride of singers and a leap of dancers, stacked behind each other in rows, with a pack of principals including Mary Costa (*Cunegonde*), Dennis Quilley (*Candide*), Laurence Naismith (*Pangloss*), Edith Coates (*The Old Woman*), me (*The Governor*), and a few others, all displayed graciously up in front. Facing us, the entire production staff and creative team without – be thankful for small mercies – the overpowering critical presence of Bernstein and Hellman. And before this intimidating mass of world-class talent, we had to read, stone cold, untutored, undirected and slightly unhinged, the libretto of *Candide*.

To make things much worse, Mary Costa had done it before, and performed and sang the whole play in full voice without a single fluff and with all the amazing *brio* of an operatic coloratura soprano in her prime. She was also very funny. And very blonde and very beautiful. I hated her. Oh, how *hateful* she was! I think I loved her really, but at that read-through I *hated* her. Her *Jewel Song*, a tour de force that very few divas could sing, let alone act, stopped the rehearsal dead and filled one person at least with a burning desire to make a swift exit. Add to this the fact that all the others were so ghastly brilliant including the singers, most of whom were moonlighting from Covent Garden chorus and sight-read the complex Bernstein score as if they'd lived with it all their lives.

February 23rd, 1959. What gets me is the way one or two of the leads act full out at the read-thro – it's almost indecent to take it so seriously.

A cold sweat gripped my heart in its pores – a lousy metaphor but it describes precisely how lousy I felt. I had my bloodless thumb in the page where the Governor entered and I flipped over the pages closer and closer to that spot with increasing dread. Closer, closer! Soon it would be time to speak! Closer, closer! It was time to speak. Closer, I *spoke*!

Everybody looked round wondering where the silence was coming from. Victor Spinetti who was sitting next to me actually looked *past* me to track it down. But I *was* speaking – well, *I* could hear me! And I must have settled in and become audible enough for the other, brilliantly enunciated voices to hear me stop so they could boom their owners' egomanias across the vast spaces of the rehearsal room. Good heavens, some of them actually seemed to be *enjoying* it! I had by now given up any thought of impressing my peers or making an impact; I was chuntering on quite fluently, laughing hugely like one of the team whenever somebody else made a mistake, and wondering rather what it was going to feel like at the end of the read-through when Bobby Lewis fired me.

He didn't.

He didn't fire me then and he didn't fire me during

rehearsals when I was worse. And he didn't fire Edith Coates either. I think I can safely say that she was as bad as me, this sweet, eccentric lady who never stopped moving, twisting and turning in restless unease as if she had a nest of hornets in her hammock. She was as dozy as I was, we both walked through rehearsals as if we'd wandered in from the street. Or been browsing through bookshops in Charing Cross Road. I don't know what her problem was, but I had never been taught to use rehearsal time the way an actor does. In revue, I would be given sketches and point numbers, these would be set, I would learn the lines and the melodies and the moves, and save any thought of a performance until I had an audience. My experience in cabaret led in the same direction. The audience made the show, *was* the show, I didn't perform for them, I performed *with* them! Now, Bobby Lewis was asking me to act just for him! *How?* To rehearse in silence, without laughter to guide me! Impossible! There was nobody else about except for the bewildered cast who must have been wondering what this gormless amateur was doing in their midst. Well, gormless perhaps, but not entirely an amateur. I was still appearing nightly at the Strand Theatre with my name very large in lights above the title of *For Adults Only*. So large, in fact, that my family used to go for a drive 'up West' on a Sunday just to take a look at it. My new agent, Sonny Zahl, Hymie's younger brother, had managed to get the managements to agree to an overlap, but the notice didn't go up on the revue until February 21st, two days before we started rehearsals for *Candide*, and two weeks before the revue actually finished.

And that may well have been why Bobby Lewis didn't fire me. He had caught me in the revue some time before and when he invited me to see him about *Candide* he said that my single in the revue, the white-faced *Pierrot at the Airport*, was 'light years ahead of the rest of the show'. Praise indeed. He redefined this praise after a week of working with me, pushing his spectacles back onto the top of his shiny bald head and murmuring: 'I haven't seen anything like this in twenty-five years.' But at least he persisted, politely and patiently, the shiny bald head never ceasing to shine with what some might interpret as thermonuclear containment.

Jack Cole worked differently. One of America's great choreographers, he was evolving spectacular routines, the kind that set the seal on the pre-eminence of the Broadway and Hollywood musical. (*February 26th, 1959 . . . watch Bobby Lewis and Jack Cole setting the 'Inquisition' scene – 'tis a joy to watch. Such efficiency and drive – I wouldn't have missed this for worlds.*) So I was impatient to work with the master. Well, six years of tap with Buddy Bradley, I thought, five years of modern dance at the Dance Centre, all those lovely routines by Michael Charnley? I wasn't Fred Astaire but the expression 'Oooh, he's a lovely mover!' was not unknown to me. I asked the great Cole when we would be setting my numbers. He didn't speak to me, he never gave the Governor of Buenos Aires any moves, he went straight back to New York after the final dress rehearsal at the Strand Theatre, and didn't even wait for the first night. Was it something I didn't say?

Bobby Lewis was something else. A master in every way. He assembled us every morning like a class at school, gave us one of his daily lectures on the status of rehearsals, where each of us was, where each of us might aim to be, how far we had adjusted to each other and what each of us needed to realise in the next phase. Then we read through and rehearsed scenes that needed work. The Director and the Teacher were one, where either began and ended mattered not a wit. It was a blessing to be part of the process.

He is the only director I have ever worked with who insisted that an actor must hang on to his script – right up to Tech Rehearsal. The script is your bible, record in it notes on your character, mark up diagrams of the blocking, have it all written down to be referred back to at those inevitable times during a run when you have lost the truth of a scene or the character and need to refresh your mind. From that time on, in every play or film I do, I treat my script as a treasured first edition, refer to it in every rehearsal, put down all the director's notes on the relevant page, not on a scrap of paper to be lost, and find time to speed-run through the entire script before every performance (matinees included) for as long as the show may run. When I'm learning the lines, I even sleep with it. Huge guffaws from actors who lose their mangled copy on the first day, dump it in some obscure corner like a forsaken odalisque? Well, laugh ye not at the Lewis school, it's a way to find new things every performance, add nuances to the character, new bits of business in a comedy, fix and polish, search for the new, fix and polish, search for the new! And it all began with Robert Lewis's note – hang on to the script.

I think the hell I went through in those days was in finding that the quick-study characters of revue, the instant impressions of that essentially two-dimensional medium, were too superficial for the musical comedy form. Given the artificiality of breaking into song in the middle of a scene, the modern musical is essentially a play and there had to be truth and deeper perception, singing or speaking, in the performance.

I was a natural clown, a mime and a mimic with no acting technique. That's why I could wait for an audience before I performed. I didn't need the rehearsal to explore and define my character and relationships with other characters. I told Bobby how I used to learn the words and music and mark the moves, and wait for the punters to guide me with their laughter before I could begin to work and build the character. Wise old Bobby listened to me – and understood. But as he pointed out on the second day of rehearsal, the other actors needed some idea of how I was going to play the Governor.

(*February 24th. He says I must not postpone so much because the others won't know how to adjust to me if I spring my character on them at performance . . . a very shrewd observation.*) I had to give them something, so I winged it as a foppish 18th century aristocrat, patronising and superior. Not the man but not bad for a start. Rehearsals could continue.

I had a wonderful time singing Bernstein's great music, especially in the quartet *Why Should I Wed?* with Mary Costa, Edith Coates and Dennis Quilley (hey, look Ma, I'm an opera singer!). But there was something missing! An Enigma rears its head! Somehow, the fop wasn't funny. Bobby suggested on the third day of rehearsal, having seen my impressions in revue, that I try it as Groucho Marx. I sunk into the familiar stoop, waved an invisible cigar, leered at Mary Costa, and got a laugh on every line. I went back to my character and got nothing! A neat little trick by Lewis, and it taught me something – they should have offered the part to Groucho!

But I was beginning, under the tutelage of the Master, to be an actor. And there was indeed an actor waiting to be born. Thanks to LSE I had worked out from the Hellman script and the original tale by Voltaire (a spirit as dear to my heart as Shaw) not only a psychological but a *sociological* concept of the Governor and I had the structural-functional jargon to prove it. Why, I not only knew who he was and where he came from, I even understood the *institutional* patterns of his *introjected* behaviour, his social *status* and *function*, his gubernatorial muscle and the power it gave him over life and death. (Please accept my apologies for lapsing from time to time into Parsonian jargon. I don't expect you to understand it any more than I do!) With such clinically perceptive tools at my command, I probed his mind, his greed, his lack of scruples in public life, his contempt for the gullible Candide, and his lust for every woman in lubricious Buenos Aires, including the frontally-endowed Cunegonde and probably even the buttockly-challenged Old Lady, whose rear had provided a rump steak, medium rare, at the siege of Azov. Here was a man of truly charismatic, Presidential potential. I understood all this and I could sing the Bflat! But I couldn't find that rat-fink Governor!

As I remember it, dear old roly-poly Bobby Lewis waited with infinite patience. And nudged and probed and shaped. And suggested. And shaped. And probed. And I had to go on every night of the four-week tour, taking on board all the notes, incorporating at second hand all the elements of Lewis's classic manual *Method or Madness*, and still, poor hopeless aspirant to the greatness beyond all endeavour, knowing there was something missing! I was in such despair the last week in Manchester that I called up my old revue mate, Vivienne Martin, clown and kindred spirit, as devoted to my work as I was to hers, ever reminding me of the essential quality of mischief that so far had always added some extra quality of magic to our work. She came up to Manchester, stayed on a few days and we spent every spare minute going through the lines and exploring the best way to do them. I applied the concept of deviation from the norm, the central theme of my work on the psychology of laughter, studied as a peripheral hobby at LSE. I split the lines down to phrases, divided the phrases into words, even made play with the syllables, then varied every nuance, accent, timbre, pronunciation and meaning of every syllable, word and phrase so that every sentence became a minefield of unexpected verbal shocks. And sure enough, every night on stage, like the tip of an iceberg with nine tenths submerged, the laughs grew from titters to chuckles to guffaws to great big gorgeous belters!

And so, as I remember it, that's how I sought and found that mystery ingredient, the character of the Governor, just as I am now seeking the mystery ingredient to account for the lack of praise in *Comedians*. That Enigma unravelled itself in

Manchester just in time for the grand opening at the Saville Theatre in London. And over that watershed in my career, over that painfully glorious plunge into the world of musical comedy, over that transition from burlesque comedian to comedy actor, stands the figure of the great Robert Lewis, Master Director, Teacher, Theatrical Philosopher, Group Theatre luminary and co-founder of the Actors' Studio, a figure of infinite kindness and compassion, so far-seeing in his wisdom that he was able to back his hunches and wait for his Ugly Duck to emerge and swan around the stage! All this is as I remember it.

And then I opened my diary!

March 12th. If only I could find a character that would fit all the farcical things this character does and yet make it credible.

March 13th. Set 'Bon Voyage'. But though it is supposed to be my number the attention is all focused on Pangloss [Martin] and Candide leaving on the rotting ship. I am practically ignored and wonder if Lewis hasn't lost faith in me . . . this is quite infuriating because I will come up later but I mustn't be produced down now! . . . It's almost as if I have started from scratch and have to prove myself.

Alas, so true! At every stage in my development, every transition from revue to cabaret to variety to musicals to plays to classics to films and back again, I have had to convince a whole new set of po-faced producers and dead-eyed directors and beer-belly bookers that I wasn't stuck for all time in my previous pigeon-hole. After twenty years listed in the top twenty London cabaret acts, my agent had a hell of a job persuading the club owners in the 70s that I could do an act. It's the name, as they say, of the game.

March 14th. *Early call again to do the Buenos Aires scenes . . . I start off by saying I am not satisfied by my lack of characterisation and suggest an accent might help. But Lewis says I should act as myself first and think about character after. What tripe! The character thinks for itself! Realise later . . . that I must just fall back on my own intuition and expect nothing from him – I was expecting some fabulous directorial treatment.*

March 15th. *Viv suddenly says do it as I had originally intended before starting rehearsals. Immediately it begins to come to life and we work out some nice ideas. What a relief! At least I feel that I have the basis of a character to develop instead of a rather obvious series of imposed attributes.*

March 16th. *Over to the Aldwych for our first run-through . . . with the help of a long black cheroot I begin to make my character tick . . .*

March 17th. *Call this morning at the Saville for Buenos Aires again – he is a dogged little bastard isn't he? Says that yesterday I was so wrapped up in my new character that I didn't come over, and he wants to read through all my stuff to get me acting it before characterising. What can I say to this man? Every character thinks and acts in different ways. In the end, after long harangues it turns out he merely wants it belted out!*

March 18th. *Generally I am pretty disappointed with my production – I have been given no business or moves – am I such a difficult person to produce?*

March 19th. *Over to Aldwych for our first non-stopping run-through . . . I go out and belt out my part and it* *comes over – two of the singers are overjoyed because I have justified their faith. I suppose some of the chorus thought I was useless. End with short talk by Bobby about divergences of style. What does he mean?*

March 20th. Bobby enlarges on his point yesterday and makes some very illuminating comments on all of us – I tend to do too much out front and not act within scene. True, I am audience-conscious. Also suggests I have more fun with the character and use lorgnette instead of cigar which is a middle-class habit – I should be an aristocrat. At costume fitting I hire a lorgnette and at 2 o/c stopping run-through, use it. He is pleased at last and at the end of rehearsal which becomes very gloomy and oppressive, he says I am cooking with gas. The company has become rather moody, probably with the strain of critical repro-ductions – I find it easier to bear because I've been having this all the time – some of the others can't take it very well.

March 21st. still quite exhausted after the gruelling rehearsals – talk about megalomaniac directors. Yet with all fairness they do work all the time.

March 22nd. My respect for Lewis is coming back the more I see him polishing and removing some of the awful performances that had crept in. Mary Costa especially needs toning down.

March 23rd. I seem to give more today and even Mary Costa says the 'Bon Voyage' is fine – the old Bflats rolled out – I do need those singing lessons each day really.

March 27th. Good Friday . . . even today (not that it is my religious concern) that little fatgut has us in to rehearse!

March 29th. On this bright Easter Sunday I finally depart for Oxford and the tour – thank goodness those awful rehearsals have ended and at last we shall have audiences. [I had booked as always at the only place in town, the Randolph] *Find most of the management and Bobby Lewis, Jack Cole, Mary and Larry here, but they all seem awfully cool – not that it worries me, but I do dislike having to start all over again . . .*

March 30th. The first night is soon upon us. And it is a great success. Mary Costa stops the show as I felt she would and Larry gets them beautifully. But my part means little; I am flat but not worried. At least I tried it his way. Am surprised to find Joan Heal, Marion Grimaldi, Hugh, Barbara and Jack all here – they think it a great show. [But no Personal Praise, not even from close friends – where have we heard that before?] *Stay up late in the Randolph discussing it all with Sonny* [Zahl, my agent] *and Viv. I only have a tiny part in this show but it isn't working out – I can't fit in with another man's timing, and they say I should suggest that I do it in my own rhythm. Oh, it is so difficult in this strange land when I just can't follow the guide.*

March 31st. 10.30 for notes – Bobby makes some very perceptive remarks, one of them being that I made up too heavily with rouge. [Osbert Lancaster did a beautiful caricature of me and Blore – Leichner's make-up expert – showed me how to do it . . . but I did too much] *Second night – and I do a virtual whiteface make-up! And suddenly I feel myself again – I cast off all the inhibitions that Bobby has set up and do it my own way – and the laughs begin to roll. Viv is delighted and so am I! What a relief! It can work. We eat in the Indian restaurant* [not the one fined for serving Kit-e-Kat in the Vindaloo]

and discuss the problems of working with a director –
I have become antagonistic towards his domination. I
need freedom to invent and experiment and last night
is proof of this! But who cares as long as I know it can
work!

April 1st. *Matinee . . . just before I am due on Peter Dalby*
[Company Manager] *comes in and says Bobby wants me*
to put my part back to Monday night. I am
dumbfounded! What sort of an idiot is this man. I do it
as I did it last night albeit a little fed up with the whole
business . . . quite sure he must have meant something
different, but when I buttonhole him later, he says I did
it like a single turn – what he means is I must connect
with the others, not do a different character. So I do it
this evening. To my surprise dear old Sonny pops in – he
had come up from London specially to see me because
Russell had told him about the trouble with Lewis [oh,
that theatrical grapevine, you sneeze in your dressing-
room, in London you've got pneumonia!] *He says he*
liked my performance tonight a lot better and saw Lewis
in the auditorium – he is willing to consider anything I
put to him but I am sick of having to refer everything to
him as if I have no judgement myself. But Sonny says it
is very important for me to make this work – it is a new
step. I agree with him of course. Good lad!

April 2nd. *. . . . at notes this morning however, I am in no*
mood for compromise and am itching for a battle. To my
astonishment he says: 'That was much better last night!'
I don't know what to say. But at least it means that some
balance has been made – now my natural timing and
rhythms fit into his pattern of production. This can free
my imagination again.

April 3rd. Photo call today so I go in at 11 o/c and make up – wait around – sit in the stalls – and find I am not needed before lunch – so off it all comes! In this mood, feeling in some way that I am being victimised, I blow up when the only photos taken are of me stuck to one side for 'Bon Voyage' . . . I tear up and tell Peter Dalby . . . when I come down, however, the photographer takes a string of close-ups, so maybe I was a little hasty. Who knows? I just know that I am not being sat on by anyone any more in this business. No sir!

As I have already mentioned, the photographer, incidentally, who may well have been intending to do close-ups of the Governor and knew nothing of the prima donna outburst in the manager's office, was a very amiable young man who was not far off marrying the Queen's sister, Princess Margaret and becoming Lord Snowdon – Tony Armstrong-Jones. I met them many times after that, backstage at all the shows they came to see, and at dinner after a special gala in Nicky Secker's Rosehill theatre in Cumbria, and they were a wonderful, warm and witty pair, bringing colour and excitement to every place and person they touched.

April 5th. Take my time leaving Oxford – as I am paying my bill I meet Bobby – there is a distinct coolness between us these days – I must say I prefer it so long as he leaves me alone . . .

The week at Bristol was uneventful, but I was still learning a lot, however much I needed to contribute myself. I was beginning to get local notices – 'a fine cameo', 'insinuating wit', 'dry sly humour', but the big deal was for Mary Costa who got raves, prompting an aside from Bobby Lewis to Jack Cole: 'I went back to tell Mary she was great – she already knew.' I wonder what he said about me.

There is an interesting entry in my diary:

April 8th. Work on the script this morning and finally begin to fix things, like where to raise my eyebrows and how to point the lines. I am beginning to get the part under control, particularly the seduction scenes. At the matinee I try out these more precise ways of giving my lines and they work . . .

So all that intensive study and breakdown of the lines, all those exercises in deviation from the norm which I had so happily remembered as happening in Manchester, actually happened two weeks earlier in Bristol. For Manchester, however, was reserved the final breakthrough, the unravelling of the Enigma of the character of the Governor! And I put everything into those last two weeks, incensed to increasing effort by a variety of things.

Firstly, the male singers were not exactly backstage buddies. One of them, whom I called Leighton Buzzard because he looked like one, looked me in the eye and blamed *Bon Voyage* on my singing rather than the production. Another, who happened to be my understudy, advised me in the kindness of his heart that I would find it easier to sing my Bflat if I constricted my throat. Realising he was unaware I had been studying voice with the great Ernst Urbach for six years, I thanked him and informed him that if I took his advice I would be off within a week. Some of the girl singers, however, rooted for me and gave me heart. Only the men were bitches.

Secondly, it was my habit on first-class tours, before and after West End runs, to stay at the best-equipped and most impersonal hotels. When your creative life is on the line, you gotta be comfortable. Digs were anathema, the thought of garrulous, overbearing, nosey landladies jawing off a hind leg when one's entire being was consumed with the solution of theatrical Enigmas, was too much. I stayed at the Randolph in Oxford, the Grand in Bristol, the Adelphi in Liverpool, and the Midland in Manchester. Now, it's a known fact that American top-liners from big-time singers to big-time directors knock up bills on tour that are likely to bust budgets, so it was inevitable that Bobby Lewis, Jack Cole, Mary Costa and lesser egotists would presume to stay at the same hotels that I did. But from the Randolph to the Adelphi they would never acknowledge that I was there.

April 14th. Go into Adelphi restaurant for meal after – and have the whole bunch of k'nuckers from the show sitting at another table and – they don't ask me to join them. What a shower of absolute bastards. I can hardly wait to see them all crawling when I am getting on. Go to bed feeling that I can't stand another minute of this ghastly nightmare – this so-called discipline that every-one says I need is a load of absolute stinking ROT! I've always had discipline of myself – my own control – it seems that they want me to shrink down to size and so lose all my creative impetus. Well, that isn't going to be!

Thirdly, we were beginning to get wake-up notices, the views of independent outsiders with no vested interest in any aspect of the production – namely, critics! The Liverpool press hit my button!

April 14th. Two papers mention the 'burlesque' and 'self-conscious clowning' of the principals – and that doesn't include me because I played it very straight – so Bobby Lewis has been keeping me down and letting the others do their nuts! Right!

Vivienne came up to Liverpool on Saturday in response to

my signals of distress. She saw both shows, made positive comments about where I had it right and I wrote:

April 18th. This is what I have been missing – perceptive direction. This bloke Lewis either doesn't know or doesn't care, probably both.

To lose faith in the Master with a week to go before town was not the happiest of portents. This Enigma was yielding up its clues in maddening fragments, the jigsaw was nearly in place and would probably be enough if I just sold what I'd got. But there was more and I had to find it that week! Manchester or bust!

April 20th. Manchester and the last week of the tour – that is something to look forward to! The first night in Manchester goes beautifully but I am still not right – still a lack of unity in my character. Back at the hotel I run through the script with Viv trying to see where it is wrong. She says I should just act it for real [an invaluable note – why did I need reminding? – when an actor is exploring his character in performance, if he is up there watching himself, he inevitably loses not only impact but truth. So 'act it for real' brings him back in line] *but I still need to fix a salient personality on it. That moron Lewis by focusing on word values and his own timing, has stopped me working (even now) from my own first principles. I must come to grips with it.*

April 21st. Up early and in for CUTS by Lillian Hellman. After great build-up, practically nothing is altered . . . second night and I do it with more attack all through – this seems to be almost it at last. I still need to fix it better psychologically but it will contain tonight's performance. Viv very pleased to have seen it finally shaping and I see her off on the sleeper back to London.

April 22nd. *I am now playing the part with consistent attack, tho' Bobby asked me not to belt out the orders to guards. Why not indeed? I am a Governor and he is a fool!*

April 24th. *With Bobby Lewis returned to London there is a new gaiety in the company – that little neurotic overshadows us all with his humourless dedication to himself. Music call this morning . . . afternoon off and a lovely day but I go back to the hotel and work on the script after lunch.*

And at last I fix the Governor's character . . .
Why this Enigma should have yielded to my dogged persistence on the penultimate day of the tour, I have no idea. I suspect it had something to do with the physical and thereby the electro-magnetic absence of Bobby Lewis, and also with the certainty that the prepared mind, the Popperian deductive method and the unceasing scrutiny of the facts *must*, sooner or later, deliver up the goods.

April 24th *(continued). And at last I fix the Governor's character – he is a bored aristocrat who always seeks new mischief to divert himself – I even have a pretended game of cards, cheating local dignitaries, to set my mood before entering. With this thought, the pursuit of fun and . nasty boy games I think I have fixed it.*

That may not seem the stuff of sleepless nights and weeks of torment, but believe me when you find your core – cool, calm and controlled – it not only gives you strategic strength throughout the whole part, but tactical spark-offs in every detail of it. Here was a man who needed to stir it up, mix it rotten and give 'em all hell because he was so bloody bored with his pampered life! Here was a man who would rob you and cheat you and send you off in a sinking ship simply because he bloody well *felt* like it! Here was a man who would ravish your women, wife, aunt, daughter or kitchen-maid, take every doxy in sight with or without buttocks, not because he was insane like Caligula or perverted like the Marquis de Sade, but because the tropical sun was beating down on the nape of his neck and he bloody well *had* to! The totally selfish, ultimate human being, *Homo sapiens* at his best-worst!

Next stop, London. The Saville Theatre. First Night.

Thursday, April 20th, 1959. *It goes very well, we are all good, but the end is greeted with boos and cheers! Well well.*

May 1st. *I sleep late then get up to find to my astonishment that I have some nice notices in the* Mail, Express *and* Times . . . Observer *and* Sketch.

Robert Robinson says: 'Performance of the evening – Ron Moody's Governor – witty, small scale, perfectly relaxed.'

Telegraph: 'The noblest leer since Cyril Ritchard fled to America.'

New Statesmen; 'Best Performance.'

Radio Critics: 'Brilliant.'

Theatre World; 'Outstanding.'

Candide ran seven weeks. The word was that Mary Costa had signed for a limited run and they couldn't find anyone else to be funny and sing an Eflat above top C. I'm pleased to record that we finished the show the best of friends with, dare I say, a hint of mutual admiration. As for dear Edith Coates who must have been at times as perilously close to replacement as I was, she also shared some of the best notices. I went to see her a year or so later in *Cav/Pag* at Covent Garden, and I was deeply impressed – and delighted for her – by the power and sheer size of her stage presence and her great contralto voice. All those restless, eccentric mannerisms that seemed over the top in rehearsal, came over in that vast Opera House as master strokes in a great characterisation. For the rest of the bunch, my diary says this on the last night:

> **June 20th**. *I suppose I have never been less concerned about the ending of any show I have done and never less concerned about the company – this is a classic on 'theatre morale' and I shall quote it in detail when I come to write my thesis* [I still hankered after that lapsed PhD] *– if ever a show went rotten from the top, this one did. Mismanaged, misproduced and miscast.*

Well, that's it! What the diary said! A personal point of view, of course, highly subjective and open to disputation by everybody involved, but only if *they* kept a diary! That fickle handmaiden, memory, makes a mockery of her mistress, history. But my very use of the diary as a source of *my* truth has thrown up a very odd and hardly comfortable contradiction. Nay, more, a veritable paradox! How could I be so abusive, letting off private steam within the privileged confines of my diary about so eminent a theatrical icon as the great Robert Lewis, and yet remember him ever after with such enormous and genuine affection? I really had forgotten, within the seven years between *Candide* and the New York premiere of *Oliver!*, that after an initial period of intense respect and awe, I had come to dislike him so intensely and written such awful things about him that I breathed blessings when he was away and ended up blaming him for what was once again, despite its success with the theatrical aficionados and the supreme talents involved, a flop! With hindsight and fifty years more experience, it's now too painfully clear. I confessed right up front to being an unschooled innocent who found his true comedic, freedom-loving soul in the fleshpots and stews of West End cabaret. I confessed that I went through hell finding that the quick-study characters of revue were too superficial for the musical comedy form. And it's clear that I had to adjust. It's also clear that my anger at the restraint and discipline needed to move on would have fallen upon the head of whoever was wild enough to handle the job. Now there's an argument for type-casting and working with old friends if ever there was! Directors have enough on their hands, and training actors is not one of them. But I was incredibly lucky. My first straight director was Robert Lewis who was also a great teacher! A highly civilised intellectual who persisted 'politely and patiently' to fit this anarchic bundle of radical talent into his highly stylised show. I was, in fact, a very lucky young man. And that's enough of the Devil's Advocate!

Now, the case for the defence!

In my fifty years in the business, I have probably worked with every kind of director in every kind of medium. Directors who are great with actors, directors who leave them alone, directors who only care about their shots, directors with a concept, directors who shoot from the hip, directors who eat too much, directors who drink too much, directors who smile all the time and drink too much, directors who curse the crew and the small-part actors and drink too much, directors who love your input to grow, directors who think you're building your part, directors who like you because you're a crony, directors who don't like you because you're the producer's crony, directors who don't like you anyway, directors who don't give you close-ups, directors who make you look great, directors . . . directors . . . directors . . .

I've managed as well as most to get on with most, but the one type of director that puts my back up is the man who directs too closely. I could quote examples of these infuriating 'sculptors' who regard you as so much clay, who practically sit on your back and creep around the set, remoulding your character with creative 'brush strokes' and 'nuances' and 'colours' and 'bridges' until you have an inordinate desire to remould the bridges of their noses with a creative bunch of colour-inducing knuckles! I'm afraid that with the same hindsight that indebted me forever to Bobby Lewis, I have to confess that he was on the fringe of this school, seeking to control the actor's transition through rehearsal into make-up into costume onto the stage into Dress Rehearsal into the First Night almost as if the poor dumb creature were incapable of thinking for himself! I wasn't actually aware of this during *Candide*, I just reacted intuitively against it. Then I read Lewis' seminal actors' manual *Method – or Madness*, a formidable work, bringing Stanislavsky's Method into American Theatre in such a way that it evolved into the Method School of Acting, breeding a whole new generation of acting stylists on the American screen. And as I read his instructions for nursing the helpless actors onto the 'stage' for the first time, coaxing them through each new phase, I wondered where they'd been all these years. For heaven's sake, we actors live on the stage, we own the stage, it's where we exist! To be fair, it may have been his intention to bottle-feed us until we had sprouted wings and then glow with pride as his fledglings took off into the true blue, award-winning yonder. I don't know, we never spoke outside rehearsals. But my passion for freedom and his passion for control had to clash!

Maybe it's the only way to learn.

Just as in *Comedians*, I had missed the boat with *Candide* and not hit strength until the last week of tour. But there was a different set of problems with *Comedians*. I was an old hand by now, classified in the blurbs as a 'veteran actor', fifty years into the business and fairly well up in all the twists and turns of the trade. This time, I didn't have to go through all the growing pains, I was happily settled into the character of Eddie Waters because I'd found him deep inside myself, within my own comedic roots. I had played Variety, the northern clubs, Butlins holiday camps, West End cabaret, I knew what it felt like to face an audience, alone on the mike, just you and them, sussing them out, switching routines to match their mood after long years of dying on your feet when the act didn't suit them and you didn't have enough tested material to change it. And I identified with Eddie's refusal to laugh at sick jokes, shared his indignation at the 'dirty-minded schoolboy stuff' that passed for contemporary humour. I was home and dry with the character! But it wasn't making the impact I knew was there to be found.

The quest for the Enigma must proceed to the next phase.

Interlude:

Memory Man, 1960

July 1st 1960. The boy who never grew up was 36 when he found himself poised on the brink of his greatest success, when the definitive stamp was about to be set on his theatrical career, when, still working mainly in theatre, much sought-after in his own brand of stand-up television, barely on the edge of film work, and all this but seven years into his busy career – he was about to make – dadada-radadaraaaa – his mark!

Oliver! opened on July 1st, 1960 for two weeks at the Wimbledon Theatre, chosen because it was a London date with no excessive touring expenses for Donald Albery, especially since the show required a stage large enough to take Sean Kenny's incomparable organic set, not to mention the huge cast of actors, singers and movers, the Dickensian set-dressings, and the atmospheric lighting – a logistic feat amounting to a wagon-load of masterclasses in all things – except our hero's memory!

He couldn't for the life of him recall – true to his ever-demanding standards – the order of the verses in Fagin's beautifully-structured, four-stanza show-stopper, *Reviewing the Situation*. To be performed as deserved, it needed to be mastered lyrically, passing well beyond mere memory-jogging tricks into that delicious flow of words from the subconscious which allows the actor to 'make it real!' But as soon as he did so, yielding to the twists and turns, the choices and caprices of the mind-changing number, he found himself in the wrong verse. Not every time! But even once a week was bad enough to frighten him silly!

He tried mnemonics and forgot the code, he tried key words and forgot the key. He thought of doffing his flat hat to read the words inside, but it was too contrived, and anyway he needed his hands free for other business. And then, surprisingly easily, he found it.

Fagin wore grey-brown woollen mittens which had the double advantage of dancing to his songs like a bunch of tatty hyperactive tadpoles, and leaving his fingers bare, front and back! So on the front of each pad of each finger of the left hand, uncovered by the mittens, went the key words!

And from this, a tiny mannerism developed, a deep-thinking, counting on the fingers habit, as if Fagin was peering hard at his left palm in 'reviewing' mode, for the resolution of his dilemma! And all the time, doing no more than reading the right word to give him the right clue to give full impact to the delivery of the stanza!

So he managed for the next six months, until one memorable day he forgot he needed a crib, found the whole routine was somehow committed thereafter to blessed memory and, until this very moment, like so many revelations in this book of constant surprises, completely forgot he'd forgotten!

10

Oliver!

After *Candide*, there came a plethora of that very same Personal Praise that had been so enigmatically missing from *Comedians* and thereby set me a-writing this short paper in search of 'why'. The sort of paper that germinates all over the place, goes far too deep into all digressions, mutates into a monographical monster, and cries out for a hardback book! Indeed, there was sufficient personal acclaim during the short run of *Candide* and after to justify, even to my own ever-doubting mind, my place upon the 'boards of the living theatre'. The six years of revue had been an apprenticeship, mad student Moody playing games with his friends, the audience! But these few months of musical comedy were somehow nearer to a real thing, another kind of Truth, the Truth of the Ahk-tor with games grown up, still playing with friends but with just a frisson of gravitas tickling the edges of the fun!

The small part in *Candide* was as important as my astute agent Sonny Zahl had predicted, the career boost was not long in taking off. Offers poured in, radio series, television guest spots, cabaret in all the West End clubs, weddings, bar mitzvahs, Music Hall with the genial Vic Oliver, an offer to host *Chelsea at Nine*, Granada's flagship Variety show, offers of leading parts in *Fings Ain't Wot They Used T'Be* and *The*

Lillywhite Boys. Fame was staring Moody right in the Bank Balance! So what did Robert Lewis's relentlessly indecisive nemesis do?

He went back to writing!

Not too surprising, I'd been writing since I was sixteen, and drawing since I was six. Short stories that I sent to *Argosy* who sent them back. Cartoons that I sent to *Punch* with equal success. And all with a leaning towards the ludicrous. Funny stuff. Laughter-making. It was in my bones! An endless outpouring of childlike ambition, to write, to draw, to paint, to sculpt, to sing, to dance, and at all times to make people laugh.

I remember as a youth of sixteen being filled with the technicolour dreams of great things to come, always great things, no modesty beneath this callow ichnography of a face, merely crushing inhibitions and tongue-tied shyness on the blushing cheeks.

I remember walking beneath the wintry night sky, watching for shooting stars to make up my mind. 'If a star shoots across on the mention of a wish, then that wish it will be!' I would say. And since I wished to bring peace to the world and go to Hollywood, I would continue: 'So what shall I wish to be, Prime Minister or film star?' And sometimes a star would shoot across on the first and sometimes on the second and I would walk home with a smile on my face and the wishes still dancing in my head.

The dream of being Prime Minister did not outlast LSE – my year as Refectory Officer on the Union Council wasn't exactly a disaster, it was more a non-event, a no-no; words like *nihil, nichts, nada* or *nebbish* come to mind.

I'd had my chance, the political route had opened up before me, the birth of a mighty rhetorician was nigh, and lily-livered, pusillanimous duck-foot that I was, I closed it. Years later when I had taught myself to speak in public, I revised my opinion, but by then the only party I could bring myself to support was the Green, and that was full of nuts. With a Government warning, no less!

Meanwhile, second choice in the shooting-star roulette passed from Prime Minister to Writer of the Great British Musical, the fond hope of scores of British writers in the face of the overwhelming American domination of the genre. Rodgers and Hart, Rodgers and Hammerstein, George Gershwin, Cole Porter, Frank Loesser, Lerner and Loewe, Leonard Bernstein, would there ever be a comparable out-pouring of genius anywhere? But that was my big ambition, I wanted to do it all, book, music and lyrics, not because it was a premonitory symptom of megalomania but because it was fun. It was my hobby! I *enjoyed* writing book, music and lyrics, way back from those early days at LSE. This has no relevance to my pursuit of the Oxford Enigma, but it does explain why I took the next few seemingly wrong steps which turned out to be right ones.

I was working full-out on a musical called *Saturnalia*, a fantasy about the great Roman Festival that predated Xmas, and was hardly receptive to anything that would take me away from it, when I received a call.

November 12th, 1959. Call from Stratford East this morning, asking me if I'm interested in a part in their new musical Fings Ain't Wot They Used T'Be, so since I want to see the Wolf Mankowitz musical now playing there, I say I'll come over this evening to talk. Go to Stratford but instead of seeing the musical I sit up in a draughty office and read the one they want me for – then I go into a long involved argument to turn it down on the grounds that it is an offensive subject which I have no liking for.

Book by Frank Norman, music and lyrics by Lionel Bart, *Fings* was of course an enormous hit because the general public, unlike puritanical me, loved 'offensive subjects' with plenty of loose women, tarts, hookers, and all other species of birds, brasses, and business ladies. There had to be, it seemed, in those days, in place of the traditional comical maid setting the scene, a mandatory 'working girl' to set the obscene, and there were scores of pretty girls with squeaky voices who could do both. But that wasn't what hooked me that day. It was that, as I was leaving the theatre I met the manager, Gerry Raffles, at the front door and we chatted awhile about theatrical things and he just happened to mention that they were thinking in their next season of doing Lionel Bart's *Oliver!* and something went *Bing!* in my head and a Merry Old Jew with a flat black hat sat down and primped his mittens in my cerebrum and awaited his moment.

I don't remember any of this; I took it all from my diary. There is no question that the device of recalling events and checking them later against the diary worked beautifully up to this moment, throwing up some piquant contradictions in my recollections of *Candide*. But from here on, it may be preferable to tell it right away as it really was, that is, by using the diaries up front as source material. This may be because there are traumatic moments in the narrative that made it harder to recall the details. For total recall clings to happy times, the 'solitary, poor, nasty, brutish and short' side of life is thrust down and back into the picky old subconscious.

Four months later, the wheels began to turn.

March 22nd, 1960. *Call from Sonny who says they want me to audition for the part of Fagin and will I collect the script today. I am not keen to audition but apparently neither Albery nor the producer saw me in* Candide *or indeed in anything so I really have no option. Go in later to collect the script from Ann Jenkins who seems nice enough . . . it is a good book and I read it while waiting for Viv to finish filming at Foley Street.*

I had a thing about auditions. A hateful public exposure of one's weaknesses. A peremptory decision made on your work before you are ready. For a character actor, it is half-conceived and half-developed, you have to vocally and physically wing it, like a chick, halfway out of its egg. No make-up to hide behind! An embarrassment. I had rarely got a job from one. Either people wanted me or they didn't want me, either they knew my work or they didn't. I was a character man, I felt I could play any character as well as anybody, but I needed time and thought to find it. What was the point in my going along there with a face like a blank canvas, without a brush-stroke of personality, waiting to be turned down because I was so damned *ordinary*? I had just done *Candide*, for heaven's sake! Didn't these geniuses at least read the papers?

> **March 23rd**. *Uncertain what to do for this audition for Fagin – finally contact Sonny and decide that the Guitar Act will at least display some comedic national characters to these first-time viewers. Also ring Ernst and he suggests I come in to* [singing] *lesson before the audition.*
>   *On to the New Theatre to do act – then I have to read a bit from the script.*

I remember this bit. The lovely old 950-seater theatre was empty except for Peter Coe, the director, Donald Albery, the Manager, and Lionel Bart, the writer, scattered around the stalls, with back-up from a pianist on stage. The Guitar Act went pretty well. Honed for years in the toughest of night clubs where it used to get belts of laughter, I believe I heard a titter or two. Then Peter Coe, who was, I have to say, very polite and clearly very interested, asked me to read from Fagin's first scene in The Three Cripples. I told him that I didn't know what to do except to imitate Alec Guinness's towering performance in the film and he said I should do that and I did and still he looked interested. He then asked me if I would sing something for them so I gave the pianist the music of *Nessun Dorma*, which was one of the arias used by Ernst to expand my voice, and I belted it out and didn't crack on the top note, at which Lionel walked out of the stalls saying 'I've seen enough!' At least he didn't say 'I've heard enough!' I was told later that Bart really wanted Max Bygraves or Sid James to play Fagin. That would have been inspired casting if he could have got Ronnie Corbett for Oliver.

March 23rd, (continued). And still that bâtard Albery isn't satisfied.

How interesting that even in those early days when I hardly knew the man, I should have sensed some quality in his nature that made me swear in French. He had all the kindliness of an income tax inspector charging you with evasion, a shard of ice suspended above your head like a Sword of Damocles. And yet I found him to be 100% honest in all his dealings. I don't think he cared about anything except a cast-iron contract for the least possible pay. I dubbed him 'Economic Man'. Perhaps I might have been more polite about him if I had realised that this was the Albery (son of Sir Bronson) who had sponsored Joan Littlewood's Theatre Workshop and produced *Beyond the Fringe* in London and New York. The man who had the sheer managerial risk-taking guts to present the first London production of the virtually incomprehensible *Waiting for Godot*.

March 23rd (continued). I restrain myself and agree to do one of the numbers from the show when Bart has written it. But I am furious at being messed around. I know I can do this part and I know equally well I cannot convince them in audition. Good in a way because it will make me concentrate on my own show and that is much more important! I don't want to help other writers when I should be helping myself.

So I wasn't *that* keen to do it! And there were other unreasonable doubts.

March 27th. *Go to see reissue of* Oliver Twist [the 1960 revival of David Lean's masterpiece] *at local Classic. And it is fascinating to see how Guinness played it about 12 years ago and established a powerful standard which it is now impossible to forget. I should like to do it but am much keener to do my own again.*

I remember walking away from the cinema having considerable second thoughts about playing such an infamous character, a fence, a poltroon, a vile corrupter of children. Could you play such a monster in a musical? And worst of all, Fagin was Jewish! What would the *Jewish Chronicle* critic say about that? What would my family say? Would I bring shame upon my mother? So it didn't worry me too much that I heard nothing for nearly a week.

April 2nd. *Call from Peter Coe. Will I come in Monday morning to do a number for him? Well, they're still interested.*

April 3rd. *Call from Sonny to say he thinks I am the favourite for Fagin. Ah, well, we shall see tomorrow.*

April 4th. *After quick lunch I go in to see Peter Coe at the Wyndham's. He seems a little vague however, and we finally end up in the New almost setting an entire scene. Then I listen to the number on tape – not bad – [it was* Pick a Pocket, *a simple tune repeated over and over]* *learn it with pianist and rehearse it with a little boy as Oliver. After all this I do the lot for Albery and though they are very pleased and full of praise* [Personal!] *they say they will let me know . . .*

Why *do* they do that? 'We will let you know!' 'Don't call us, we'll call you.' All these pithy little phrases that give you a short, sharp shock in the pit of your vulnerability, verbal instruments of torture fiendishly wielded to keep you swinging on the short, sharp hook of 'vaulting ambition' – that is if – and I do say if – you *really* want to do the show! Round and round in your head go the paranoid doubts! Who didn't want me? Which one was sticking out for somebody else? *Bart hates me, I'm sure! . . . But what if Coe hates Bart . . . and Albery hates them all? . . . And Bart wants Danny Kaye . . . and haven't I got better things to do?*

April 6th. Call from Sonny this morning – Albery, his secretary and Peter Coe all thought I did a beautiful audition and they want me to do Fagin. Well, well. I am very pleased though I still don't want to do the show for Bart. Sonny has asked £150 [a little less than I got in Adults] *which still seems to me a fair figure.*

April 8th. Sonny tells me that Albery has offered £85 and a year's get-out – what bloody sauce. I suggest that we make it £100 and nine months as an absolute minimum. It seems to me that this Albery is a right bastard. [In English!]

There I go again, maligning fine theatrical figures in the privacy of my diary! Blasts of venom tenderized by time into fond memories! So why bother to get upset? Another diary entry on this day deserves a mention.

April 8th, (continued). Collect Viv . . . go to see Les Enfants du Paradis, *the film that made such an impression on me so many years ago – but then the mime meant little to me. Now it means so much and I realise what a superb mime Barrault is, in his impression of Deburau. Ah, such inspiration.*

April 9th. Call Sonny later this morning to find out what has developed – he has just finished another hour's lecturing by Albery on the economics of the theatre and why he will not alter his offer. What an absolute sod! So it has come to the final decision – do I do it or not? Because I am quite confident that Albery will not budge and would rather have a second choice of artist than yield on terms. A tiny little tyrant who feeds off his victories. In view of my reluctance to do this show at the expense of 'Saturnalia' I am afraid I shall have to turn it down.

April 11th. Dreadful day of indecision. Sonny tells me Albery has awful reputation with all who deal with him, but that is why his shows pay off. We shall see. Passover begins tonight and we are already eating matzo.

So many times over the years, the Jewish Festival of Passover has coincided with drastic developments in my life, dilemmas over work, heartbreaks over girls, all kinds of complex problems to resolve, almost as if, apart from the pious state of mind required for the Festival, one has in the traditional Passover Seder service a kind of meditation, where the father reads the story of the Exodus mostly in Hebrew, and the mind is thereby able to wander to its problems and be, more often than not, blessed with a solution. In view of the dazzling ingenuity of the ground rules of Judaism, I like to believe that is part of its purpose.

April 13th. Viv and I discuss it and she points out that with Fagin and even a year's run, I can rewrite 'Saturnalia' and get it set up whilst building my name. So it is wisest to do Oliver! *and even though Albery wins this time, the wheel always turns. Yes! This morning I ring Sonny and tell him I will do it! He agrees and thinks it is a part that will establish me as a leading ACTOR. Hm. Very relieved and so is Mum. Go on to Viv's and tell her I have accepted and she too is happy and relieved. She felt I had to do it. Women! How do they always know these things?*

And that was that! Once again I did something by the skin of my teeth, nearly passed over a major turning point in my career, but when you think how I nearly didn't come into show business at all, it's hardly surprising. Sad to admit there is no elegantly perceived Enigma, Truth, Serendipity or Paradox in this observation, merely bumbling indecision and a dash of resentment. In the following few weeks I appeared on radio, in cabaret and on television, non-stop, with a great deal of Personal Praise in all areas, and developed a taste for Grand Opera thanks to Ernst Urbach, my singing teacher, who got the tickets, and it wasn't till May that the slumbering Leviathan, *Oliver!*, stirred once more in its sleep.

May 3rd. Have to call in at Wyndham's to check the key for my numbers in Oliver! *The main single, 'Reviewing', though derivative of 'Yiddisha Momma', is still very strong and interesting. I think this part has a lot of potential – I wonder how it will work out in production?*

The musician, incidentally, who set the keys was Martin Goldstein, brother of Wally Goldstein, one of the happy bunch of Jewish intellectuals who had seemed to be behind so much of the student entertainment and publications at the

London School of Economics. Well, it's a small world.

> **May 4th**. *I suppose I ought to begin work on* Oliver! *but I can't bring myself to try – I'll just have a few days' holiday and go into this thing cold and see what happens, because I am going to have a lot of thinking to do and I shall want help from Peter Coe and Lionel Bart before deciding on the character.*

So I collected Vivienne and off we went in Lulubelle, my open-topped Consul Convertible, off on the road to ANYWHERE! In fact it was an idyllic holiday in the West Country, Bath, Cheddar Gorge, Torquay, Babbacombe, and then we started back, we happy pair, with our truckles of Cheddar and clotted cream caramels, to discover that my sister had had a baby boy that day and I was an uncle!

> **May 9th**. *And so off I go for the first day of rehearsals of* Oliver! *– at the Mary Ward Settlement where dear old* Candide *had its growing pains. This is quite a large company after all and the dozen tiny lads fill the place up – this is going to be a right lark working with them. We do a read-through which I find less embarrassing than before and I do it mainly à la Guinness – except in the numbers which I do more as myself. And get some laughs! Well, well! But it seems a happy set-up and Peter Coe is a friendly, relaxed director so I shall watch developments with interest. Georgia Brown, playing Nancy, is nice to work with at the moment – I still wish it had been somebody a little less intense and heavy.*

Established as a jazz singer of note who had borrowed her name from the old standard, *Sweet Georgia Brown*, Georgia had come to fame as Lucy in the 1956 revival of Kurt Weill's *Threepenny Opera* in London and off-Broadway.

I am astonished to find no mention in my diary of the model set which Peter Coe and Sean Kenny, the designer, took great delight in showing us on the first day. I can't believe I didn't write anything because I thought it was the greatest set I had ever seen, an organic structure which – apart from a painting of St Paul's and environs, à la Daumier, on the back wall – consisted of a series of interacting, reinforced wooden blocks that moved around each other, driven by a stage-hand seated within, creating new forms and patterns, with small set pieces moving in to define the setting. It was a set that could have had a permanent place in any theatre, a masterpiece of limitless potential that could encompass everything that Shakespeare wrote and everything he didn't. I don't remember if that was the moment I told Sean Kenny, with his cherubic smile, that he was a genius, but it was certainly the moment I had a vague sense of what it was like to be present at the birth of a fantastic history-making hit. And I still think that if somebody with a theatre could install Sean's set today, they would never have to spend another penny on scenery!

May 9th (*continued*). *Home early to do some reading and thinking about Fagin, though I don't want to anticipate too much. I'd like to know why Peter Coe wanted me and what he saw in me and build from that – the days of impressions are past – no more imitations of other people's mannerisms but development of new styles. Anyway, I had to do it, didn't I?*

May 10th. *Talk to Peter about the character this morning and he tells me to do it as* myself *for the time being and then build from that. Just what dear old Bobby Lewis tried to tell me – I think I may find this show less of a battle because the hard battle was in the first conflict with Lewis – and he did me more good than I could ever* *have known. Doesn't it make one humble to realise one has always so much more to learn. Spend most of day learning music under Bart's supervision – this is his big opus so I hope he succeeds. I feel a sort of identification with him.*

__May 11th__. Call today for music again, and I find it very easy to learn, surely because he writes his tunes in his head and they are not complex. Gives me a great deal of confidence in my methods – but I am not thinking of 'Saturnalia' now – this job is the main thing and I must make sure I do it well.

Albery comes in and tries to be friendly but I am rather short with him. I can't forget his unfair deal. But I have to do this part so it's no good harbouring grudges – that is just a waste of energy . . . one always has a chance to turn things around in this cockeyed business. [That brings to mind the ancient aphorism: 'Be nice to people on the way up, because you meet them all on the way down!' And never forget the famous line: 'A pain in the neck is worth two in the crutch.']

__May 12th__. In this morning for a general read and sing-through of show for Lionel to see how it shapes up – it is very good and it is a neat job. He is very pleased and they all think I am doing fine though I have as yet no idea at all of the character. It's strange actually how I feel about this whole show because I resent having to do it and even more so under the conditions that I accepted from Albery.

I think he made a mistake driving too hard a bargain, and he must have known because he finally contracted to pay me £95 a week. A whole tenner more! That must have hurt!

As for Bart, he was so open and friendly, I wished him well.

But having last worked on *Candide* where the incredibly literary Lillian Hellman/Stephen Sondheim script was jam-packed with witty lines and exemplary lyrics, Bart's script seemed rather too evenly spaced, even sparse, with short bursts of dialogue alternating with a page or two of lyric. We soon discovered, however, that this simple balance played incredibly well. And Bart's material was very easy to learn – and there was plenty of space for ad-libbing, in case any member of the cast should dare to be so outrageously inclined. Or, may I say it, gifted? Sparkling *bon mots* do not come easily! But please don't accuse me of indulgence. Firstly, it wasn't me; it was Fagin up to his tricks! Secondly, words might be needed because there was something wrong with the dialogue. A mini-Enigma, easily solved! I went through Fagin's chapters in *Oliver Twist*, painstakingly comparing them to Bart's script, and to my horror I found that small changes had been made in Dickens' unique style, establishing a kind of wash of cockney modernity over the master's golden prose! Magnificent period words that were the very essence of the Age of Victorian melodrama had been diluted into charmless, watered-down Dickens-Bart! In the book, Fagin's lines were loaded with character and rich colour. 'Drop' was a word for 'gallows' and 'peach' was a word for inform. In the musical 'How d'ya do?' presumed to replace: 'I hope I shall have the honour of your intimate acquaintance?'

So I quietly put Dickens back into my script!

I left alone the lyrics (or as Bart called them, 'songwords'), made no changes in anyone else's lines, played Dickens' words, ad-libbed as Dickens would have ad-libbed, protected and sustained Dickens all through rehearsal, all through performance, and seven years later, all through the film . . . and nobody ever noticed!

And what of Bart's music?

May 12th (continued). *He is no marvel and all his tunes are derivative, some incredibly so, but he is workmanlike and clear cut in his decisions.* [How strange to read that opinion fifty years later, when the entire score has been enshrined in the archives of musical comedy greats.]

As for Georgia, it soon became clear that she *was* Nancy, or at least one of the ways of playing her, a real tough cookie rather than a simple-minded waif; a rough street smart who could flatten a man with a straight left rather than, perhaps, a warm-hearted, knees-up cockney; a quasi-baritone belter rather than a *Salad Days* soprano. I found it hard to warm to her even though we shared the same Semitic roots, something that had till then always formed an unspoken but familial bond. She was obviously a great mate of Lionel, behaved as if she had a special status in the show, while he clearly wanted it to be a big hit for her. Great, I understood that, I felt the same way about Viv's career. I just wanted this to be a happy show!

And happily indeed, my memories of the rehearsals of *Oliver!* were of lovely sunny days, rehearsing in Wimbledon, admiring Lionel's Mercedes coupé (well, he was a big-time rock composer!), pub lunches with the cast – enjoying the work – and getting used to the hordes of very small boys aged between 8 and 10 who appeared amongst us most days of the week exhibiting the most incredible amount of energy. I think we had twice the number of imps that we needed because of some law about ringing the changes so that you never knew which diminutive face was going to appear at each performance. They rehearsed all their scenes and numbers full out under the steely eyes of their chaperones – they sat patiently when they had to – in their lunch break they were very quiet while they fed – and then bursting out of whatever unseen restraint was holding them (and this, for about fifty minutes) they ran around the rehearsal room, playing and yelling like a horde of pygmies with a touch of the sun. One of the chaperones said that the boys were able to keep up the action all day, singing and dancing and yelling, and when they got home, went up to bed and out like a light!

May 14th. Call this morning for more work on 'I'd Do Anything', which is a very catchy number set in a very charming way, spinning parasols as wheels on a carriage. Clown stuff, no less! I am enjoying these rehearsals and find the kids (and Georgia) easier to work with than I had anticipated. I'm still not trying to be definite about the character, but mainly being my own mad self and having fun. [Well, listen to me, now happily doing what maestro Robert Lewis tried to instil into me in *Candide*, but no longer clinging desperately to the ways of revue and instant characterisation just because that was what I was used to!]

Back home I begin [for the first time] *to read the whole of* Oliver Twist [over length and oh, so much larger than life] *and it is entirely fascinating. I haven't read Dickens for so long, and find the flavour refreshing and vital, though a little wordy, a little soggy with figures of speech, and typified especially with over- and under-statements which give the whole an air of satirical comedy . . . reading it is a very enjoyable by-product of my new job. And the lesson is clear, for players of Dickens as well as Shakespeare – they both need cutting!*

All sweetness and light? Not quite . . .

May 16th. Rehearsing in earnest now – this time 'Pick a Pocket' with the kids, when we first build up the comedy sequences in mime (and Peter encourages my comedic input) and then fit in the verses. I enjoy the first part, but find that the words as written are not going to fit the movements, which to me is fuzzy producing and should kill both . . . but they are quite happy . . . I am sure it is wrong.

May 17th. First feelings of dissatisfaction this morning when we rehearse the second Thieves' Kitchen scene where Oliver is returned – and I find to my horror that it is being played hard and heavy, and Georgia is doing the full hysterics! And Peter doesn't want any comedy in it at all! Well, well, we shall have to see about that! Laughs grow in fertile soil – you can't kill natural growth! I point out that I have just done a light comedy number – 'Reviewing', – so how can I be tough and sinister after that? And he says leave it for now – so he obviously hasn't thought about it! Well! We're here to think!

Further upset when Joan Thring [publicist] comes in with the Press photographers to have publicity for Georgia and the kids. What is this, the Georgia Brown show? They don't want Moody and we haven't started yet? Ah, well, it's the notices that will count, so I must just concentrate on working hard!

Now that I look back I do see the steady build-up, from the very beginning, of an ominous tsunami of *tsouris* (which is quasi-Yiddish for big trouble), and will soon enough yield, within these pages, another variation on the redoubtable Enigma. See if you can spot it!

May 18th. Further alarm this morning when I find the 'Three Cripples' scene is also played heavy, and I am beset with the giggles every time I act with Dodger who is worse than me. If he keeps up this way, Peter will have a melodrama on his hands and not a musical comedy . . . and indeed I feel that he has no feeling for comedy as witness the confused production of 'Pick a Pocket'. Hm, this show isn't going to be as straightforward as I thought – the old battle is in the offing! Shades of Candide *in so many ways.*

Nathan's later, for very messy and indecisive costume fitting in which I am covered in old tat and nobody seems to know what is wanted!

May 19th. Move into the Prince's for rehearsals and find they have erected a massive superstructure for the set, which can be moved by hand – the actual set will be a great mass of beams and levels, driven by a motor. And that at least should be something to see! Set the Three Cripples scene with the whole company and it is quite effective en masse.

Interesting to recall Jack Cole's masterly, pre-plotted choreographic patterns in *Candide*, contrasting with Peter Coe's almost casual method in *Oliver!*, virtually throwing the actors in and telling them to take up their natural positions around the benches and tables of the pub, before shaping them into a final dramatic pattern. Cole's work, drama on the edge of dance; Coe's work, dance on the edge of drama. Two men, two experts, two methods – oh, how I love this business!

May 19th (continued). After lunch we rehearse a new number that Lionel has written for me and the boys to close the first half ['Be Back Soon']. *Good – that's what I like to see! Lionel's a good lad! And it is a gay, bright number too, as they whistle their way out, and I levitate round and about and off in my spontaneous pas de basque and wonder what happened to gravity!*

May 23rd. Am relaxing at home, ready for The Barber of Seville *this evening when I am suddenly called for evening rehearsal! I protest furiously and ring Peter Coe but the bearded bastard won't budge! So I have to collect Viv and let her go on while I go in dressed up for the opera* [the Grand Tier, no less!] *to do a lousy rehearsal on The Three Cripples! Am furious but don't refuse to rehearse! And suddenly, after we have run it a few times, Peter tells me to buzz off!*

It was only then, running through the crowded streets from the Prince's Theatre to arrive, breathless and sartorially crumpled, at Covent Garden just in time for the opera, that I realised what that crafty, conniving Coe had done. He had got what he wanted! He'd got me so mad, I didn't giggle with Dodger! Come to think of it, Dodger didn't giggle with me. We'd both had a lesson in rough acting. Dodger was played by Martin Horsey, a very smart young man and we got on famously together, but he didn't know why Peter had suddenly sent me bananas! When I shook Dodger by the lapels, I really shook him by the lapels! You should have seen his face. When I threw Dodger's coat across the floor, followed by Dodger, I really threw them across the floor! He thought I'd gone mad. Well, I was mad in the bone! And Coe knew that you can't act mad unless you have it in the ulna – you have to feel it! However much of a clown Fagin might be, a mushroom cloud of panic would explode within him at the merest threat of the 'drop'. The deep, deep dread that if Oliver 'peaches', they're all dead! A whole piece of Fagin's character had fallen into place. Not to mention Dodger's. And from then on we really enjoyed doing that scene – without angling for laughs. Although there was always some sicko in the audience who thought it was funny. Incidentally, *The Barber* that night was a masterpiece.

May 23rd (*continued*). *Wonderful to see such inspired clowning in an opera by the original Italian company! Suddenly see all its origins in the Commedia del Arte.*

One of the nights we shall treasure.

May 25th. *Early call for 'Be Back Soon' at the Prince's – I am not completely happy with the rather ordinary setting of this, and feel that we should cover it with a 'Pied Piper' theme to counteract the Fagin figure* [just as I laid in Deburau's 'walking on the spot' to link the verses of *Pick a Pocket* and the lightening leaps and lip-licking excesses of Joe Grimaldi to keep you wondering what the unpredictable clown would do next.] *This way, by linking Fagin with other great figures of literature I can help to soften him and extend him and give him a quality outside that of Dickens's monster. What we might call The Pied Piper Variation is perhaps the most valuable slice of serendipity I have stumbled on so far.* [What you might call, cross-breeding character. Or theatrical mix and match.]

Back for rehearsals of second 'Thieves' Kitchen', the one scene that upsets me because it is so intense, and Georgia keeps having the full hysterics even in rehearsal. Is all that necessary? It's unpleasant. Makes you feel sorry for Bill Sykes.

I don't like to leave those words unattended on the page, though that is clearly what I felt at the time, and our assessment of the *Oliver!* imbroglio must stay with the true state of affairs. Here comes dear old Truth again! I just didn't take to Georgia. It happens in shows. A show is like a small village with gossiping neighbours and overhanging branches and you know what *they* do! And here's another thought, however unlikely: maybe she just didn't like me! Hey, maybe, with such intense feelings at play, we were meant to fall in love. My mother would have been pleased, but she thought Georgia was Lionel's girlfriend. Oy vais! It's only a show! Let's sort it out later.

11

Fagin

May 26th, 1960. Over to Prince's for a wasteful evening rehearsing that slice of nauseating melodrama-cum-method, the second 'Thieves' Kitchen' scene. I really believe that Georgia finds a cathartic release in this scene. And Peter Coe keeps jumping on me for fear I should make it funny – my whole conception of the part is funny – if Fagin becomes real he becomes sinister and I must eventually stick to my guns. Meanwhile we shall go along with it and see what develops.

With *Oliver!* I was facing a different set of problems from those of *Candide*, where the whole piece was a witty satire with overtones of American burlesque. *Oliver!* was pure tragi-comedy, *mit Moody stück*, ranging from laughter to tears. It was early days to be certain who was right, laughs come in the most unexpected places and we needed an audience to judge where they would fall.

May 27th. Day off, so I get down to reading more of Oliver Twist – I've always believed that I'd read it before but now I'm sure I haven't – must have been the film and other potted versions that made the story so familiar. Also, Fagin, though called 'The Merry Old Jew' is actually painted by Dickens as an insidious monster who corrupts young boys to crime – and I find that this reading is not helping me at all. Unless I can compromise by changing the INTERPRETATION of the FACTS that Dickens presents. So Fagin was a crook – but why paint him in such evil colours? Bart's lyrics and music have already gone a long way towards humanising the old goat and I will surely be up there hoofing alongside him on the peaks of merriment!

May 28th. *Do very useful call on 'Reviewing' later – it is finally taking shape along the lines I suggest, that is, Fagin is about to run away but keeps being drawn back. Well, that's it; I have set all the stuff I am in.*

Although not totally improvising in that we always worked with a choreographer to give form and style to solo numbers, most of us in revue became highly skilled in setting our own singles. This hadn't applied to *Candide* where my musical items were set virtually in concert. *Why Should I Wed* was four of us in a straight line, in some kind of minimalist mobile minuet (Edith Coates didn't need setting, remember? She never stopped moving); *Bon Voyage* had everyone in transit, and me glued to the spot! (I never saw choreographer Jack Cole again after the show ended, but then I never really saw him during it. Not one move or word did he give me! Maybe he was shy? *Gevalt!*)

When Malcolm Clare and I set *Reviewing*, we both stood back and let Fagin take over. I wasn't aware I had an iota of his character yet, but then I didn't realise how deep inside me he already was, how deep right down to my very own ethnic roots. That is, so much Truth in Performance was already there. Bart knew it; we shared the joy of his creation. Coe must have seen it at the audition, he just hadn't realised he was opening a Pandora's Box of comedic anarchy. And Fagin knew it because he went right in there and told us what to do with the lyric! Go off a little further up Sean Kenny's enticing stairs on every decision to leave, come back down a little faster to Sean Kenny's safe and cosy fireside on every terrified return!

Peter Coe didn't think it was a funny number, but a serious soliloquy. I knew it was funny, but I didn't know where the laughs were. Oh, I *do* love this business!

June 1st. We are working very long hours on this show. But nobody minds that. I am more terrified of wasted rehearsals and inefficiency, and nobody can find that in this set-up. 'Three Cripples' (not my favourite scene) and 'London Bridge' (my easiest) and then I nip off for a singing lesson with Ernst. What would I do without him to keep my voice up to scratch?

What indeed would I have done without Ernst Urbach? 'Ronnie,' he said to me once when I hit top C in exercises, 'if I had had you earlier, you could have been an opera singer!' Maybe that is why most of my rehearsal pieces were operatic arias like *In Fernem Land, Che Gelida Manina, Nessun Dorma*, all testing pieces with high tessituras. I gave my greatest performances whilst taking a bath, and I suppose the best compliment I ever had was when I was belting out *Che Gelida* one time in a hotel bath, and a voice a few doors away yelled, 'Switch off that bloody radio!'

So where did Fagin find his singing voice? From Ernst, of course. And from my love of the might and passion and purity of an operatic voice. And because I saw a musical film once where a huge, fat pirate sang his rather ordinary song in an extraordinary tenor and ennobled the whole film. And because I will never forget another film in which Reginald Gardiner, that brilliant English comedian famed for his train impressions, played a deliciously snob-soaked butler who, having been deeply offended, walked out into the gardens, sang a wondrous aria in a thrilling tenor voice, and suitably set at ease by this cathartic release, straightened his tie and strode back in.

All the stuff of show business, all the wonders of heaven to chose from. So I gave Fagin – or should I say Fagin gave me – an operatic voice. Could this be bending one of the many Truths in Performance? Maybe, but nobody has ever commented on it. Lionel Bart (who would have been happy to hear Max Bygraves singing 'You gotta pink a toothbrush or two, boys') never questioned my timbre or my cadenzas. But a few times, when I went a little too far singing Oliver to sleep and rolled in a few Kosher appoggiaturas, it was suggested on most nights save Fridays that I might apply for a cantorial post in the local synagogue.

__June 1st__, (continued). Am invited to the Dress Rehearsal of a new revue tonight. Oh, dear, oh, dear, what a mess it all is, and how bad the management. I am glad to leave and actually find myself thanking heaven for Donald Albery and the sheer professionalism of Oliver! *even in rehearsal.*

__June 2nd__. Early call at Bermans for my costume which is a great cape made of Harris Tweed – I shall dissolve in the hot weather. What a silly idea – ah, well, stupidity creeps in in the best of circles and winter is coming – in about six months!

More rehearsals on the 'Thieves' Kitchen' which are taking shape each time – I am still reading from script and don't know my numbers, but I suppose that will be OK on the night.

__June 3rd__. Call in on Anello and Davide to select pair of brown leather mediaeval shoes to keep in with the Pied

Piper theme – I know they are out of period but it is a touch I need in the character.

In fact I was actually sent to Anello's to fit a pair of Victorian shoes, was ushered down into the basement, saw the mediaeval shoes that just happened to be lying on the floor and *grabbed* them! *Mine*! Serendipity had spoken, who was I to resist such a twist of fate! They were lying on the floor, egad, who *put* them there for heaven's sake? Well, now, what would Bobby Lewis have said about that? What a battle I would have had to persuade him that I *needed* mediaeval Pied Piper shoes to nudge Fagin out of his sordid Victorian mould with its overtones of anti-Semitism! Inverted prejudice, you say? No Truth in it? Well, let's just guess that Fagin bought them in a Turkish market! A succulent bite of Turkish Delight! I needed them, just as I needed Fagin to sing with an operatic voice to set the seal on a kind of dignity, and needed Fagin to take Marcel Marceau-type mime steps to tie him in with the universal clown that was beginning to reveal itself through his persona. Fagin was growing within me, drawing all the threads together, I felt like a wizard waving a wand, creating a force field that pulled in puffs of magic and sparkles of fun, and influences, and sub-texts, all coming in together, a confluence of quips and quirks, with most of all, right at the heart of it, a dynamic, Deburau-esque, Grimaldi-esque, Chaplin-esque, naughty, naughty, naughty spinal tap of MISCHIEF!

What would Bobby Lewis have said about all this if it didn't fit in with his Method and his Madness because it was rooted in the mischief of the clown rather than the gravitas of the actor? I rather think he would have approved. But whatever he might have said, I would merely have yelled the magic word: SERENDIPITY!

Serendipity! Discovery, for the prepared mind, by happy accident. Just one of the ways Fagin was revealing himself, little by little, as a clown, an inventive, shtick-seeking comic, an archetypal laughter-maker who attracted lost boys to live his life, because, as we all know, little boys are born to be naughty! And – while safe inside the Thieves' Kitchen with Fagin, their natural soul mate, they could smoke and drink like little old men – outside in the Market Place, with Dodger masterminding tactics, they could rob the rich and never, never, never – 'cause if you do it's your own damn fault get caught!

Serendipity! Discovery by happy accident! Like the magic moment when Fagin takes the parasol from Nancy in 'I'd Do Anything' intending to do no more than twirl it as he pirouettes on the coda, then, being a clown who never gives up a prop while it's still breathing, clings to it without the faintest idea why! Until he's into 'Be Back Soon', and the parasol transmogrifies into a flute in his hands, and he is the Pied Piper dancing a *pas de basque*, and leading the line of boys up and around and away to take Oliver off on his first job! Where did that come from?

Serendipity! Discovery by happy accident! Like the first Wednesday matinee when Fagin opens his treasure chest for 'A cuppa coffee and a quick count-up!', and discovers the dumb Assistant Stage Managers have, for the first time, put in a money bag of gold coins, tied at the neck! What does he do? Rattle it? Sniff it? No! He whips open the bag, pours the hoard of cash into the lid top, counts down six coins to the lid bottom and sweeps the six across, all with the staccato crash of a machine-gun – *dada dada dada crash! dada dada dada crash!* over and over and over, sending the old dears, (who are really only here for the cucumber sandwiches) into a crescendo of laughter! Where did that come from?

Since we are now deep in clown country, we might do well to mention the equipage for the badinage, the appurtenances for the impertinences, the gags for the gigs, the tools for the fools, what we might call the stock-in-trade for the shtick-in-trade, the facilities for the farcilities and the etcetera for the theatera! When, as I have already noted, I first read the script of *Oliver!* it was a bit like (but not quite) reading that! Bart had altered Dickens' phraseology into something that was meant to be more comprehensible to a modern audience. And I'm afraid, as I said, following my natural instinct, the unforgiving purist in me went carefully through the original and put it all back! Naughty purist! But *then*, naughty clown! What he didn't tell you was that he added gags in the style of the master, for the deliciously underhanded purpose of getting laughs! And who got the credit? Not Moody, he merely wanted the show to work! Dickens and Bart got the credit!

Bart came in to see me after we had opened in the West End and demanded that I stop ad-libbing; the lines must be put back to the way they were on the first night. I merely informed him that there were no laughs on the first night and if I hadn't added the funny lines, there wouldn't be any laughs, and we couldn't try them until we got the audience. He didn't complain after that. And the lines stayed in all through the run and into the film. There's a nice little Enigma I think I have solved – how to bring the classics up to date without changing a word. Just adding a few!

> *June 5th. Begin to really work on the script and analyse the development of Fagin through the show . . . I think I've found the clue to his character in the Three Cripples scene – where the old Jew, a lonely man who must have had a hellish childhood of snubs and insults, is accepted as one of the thieves, indeed as their kingpin.*

There is no anti-Semitism in Dickens' underworld, there are no masterly portraits of insinuating snobs or racist hypocrites or rabid xenophobes to luxuriate in such deceit! Nobody spits on Fagin as Bassanio spits on Shylock in *The*

Merchant of Venice and is actually encouraged to do so in the script.

It has to be mentioned, however, that the character of Fagin is anti-Semitic by default. That is, Fagin is described again and again as 'The Merry Old Jew', though he is by no means merry, nor is he a Jew in ethnic terms. Apart for a few 'my dears', which is a universal term of affection, Fagin does not demonstrate any ethnic traits that could define a Semitic nature. His idiosyncratic costume and flat hat hints at His Excellency the Cardinal of Hackney, and is more likely the invention of Cruikshank, the great caricaturist, whilst the monstrous hooked nose would better suit a Berber in the Sahara Desert. And yet Fagin, the fence and malignant 'corrupter' of children, is called 'The Merry Old Jew' simply because it was the custom in those days to call a fence a Jew even if he was in fact a Moslem, a Southern Baptist or an Indian fakir! But then (as Jimmy Durante might so nasally have put it), 'If you're gonna have a nose, have a nose!'

I had by now pinned down most of the Truths in Fagin's persona, laced with one or two harmless flimflams, like the mediaeval shoes and the operatic voice and it was now time to pin down Truth in Performance! I went to LSE to see my old psychology tutor, Professor Hotopf, for advice. Since *Oliver Twist* was written in 1838, what kind of man would Fagin have been? Hotopf felt that since the Russian and Polish Jews came to England in 1900, and the German influx was in the 1930s, Fagin in 1838 would have been an English Jew with probably a heavy London accent. What we now think is a Jewish accent was, in fact, developed by Russian and Polish immigrants much later. All the same, I couldn't resist adding a schmeckel (you should excuse the expression) of Yiddish to Fagin's voice, a heimishe inflection, a hint of that marvellous klezmer music in the words that Leo Rosten has so brilliantly demonstrated in *The Joys of Yiddish*.

In addition to all this I was able to conjure up a paradigm case, a magnificent concrete example of a real life Hebrew teacher, not remotely dishonest but an incredible controller of rough and ready Tottenham boys. Mr Tomback was his name, and he was right out of Dickens! And when Mr Tomback flicked his yamulka, or prayer-cap, on the back of his head and wagged his finger and clipped the ear of a boy unaccustomed to doing as he was told . . . that boy did as he was told! Tomback, as Secretary, not only controlled the boys, he controlled the Shul (synagogue)! He was in charge! And when I stunned Fagin's Boys with a roar of 'Drink up yer gin!' or 'Let's show Oliver 'ow to do it, my dears!', I gave out every nuance of every Truth but none quite so much as that of the incomparable Mr Tomback! My grandparents and mother and father were all founder members of the Tottenham Talmud Torah, the totally orthodox local synagogue that served the ethnic and spiritual needs of the hordes of tailors and hair-dressers and grocers who had turned North London into a mittel European ghetto. I was still a member, always supporting the old Shul on Yom Kippur, until it closed for lack of support a few years ago. That's where I spent my traditionalist childhood, my agnostic undergraduate years, my ancient of days of true belief, and that's where I got the Truth of my background and my way of life and eventually, twenty-four years later, the Truth of the heart and soul of the prototype of Charles Dickens' Merry Old Master Pickpocket. Sometimes you just have to wait.

June 6th. Set Finale today – and in spite of some tension from dear Miss Brown, I enter last and am placed in the middle of the line-up . . . music call at the Prince's – always an enjoyable time because one hears the orchestrations for the first time – and Eric Rogers has done a magnificent job on these, utilising a miniature symphony sound – and also because everybody, including the producer, relaxes and has plenty of time for tea.

June 7th. *Down to Wimbledon this evening for run-through of first half in the set – and what a set! Absolutely fabulous piece of work like a great wooden mobile of jagged timbers turning with superb ease and re-shaping into new settings to give the whole production an unusual flow. Well, well. This is really something, whatever happens to the rest of the show. Visit Viv after and work on the script with her – I don't know what I'd do without her enthusiasm and help.*

June 8th. *Early call at Berman's for fitting today . . . I am not at all pleased with the monstrously heavy cloak they are wrapping me in, but what use is it to protest with this bunch? And anyway I always have an uncertainty about sticking too firmly to my own guns – one can get so many new ideas through adapting oneself to necessities and limitations.* [Flirting, perhaps, with Serendipity?]

Peter said he wanted a triangular coat to give Fagin stability, with an eye-catching brown rather than a swallowed-up black, and a flash of red kerchief at the neck. And in the end, with the flat, black cardinal's hat, and the master-stroke mittens, throwing the fingers into relief, and of course the mediaeval shoes that nobody ever mentioned, who could say Cruikshank's etching hadn't come to life?

June 10th. FIRST NIGHT, WIMBLEDON, *is very successful all in all, and the visitors are very complimentary. Ernst thinks I am wonderful but doesn't like the show. Viv overjoyed, and that's what counts. Thelma* [Ruby] *in, and invites us back to her house for some food. Bill Boorne,* [*showbiz critic of the* Evening News], *is already there* *smiling inscrutably. (But letting it be known that the show is something special.)*

June 11th. *The matinee is awful, but the second house is lovely and our first real audience. I get laughs all through, ad-libbing where the lines haven't stuck – a very prudent survival technique. Even in the heavy scene a few are squeezed out of the intensity set up by Madame Brown – yes, she set up the laughs! I mean, what about when I said: 'Why Nancy, you're wonderful today! Such talent, such an actress!' What a laugh! I was more surprised than she was! I wasn't even trying to be funny! (He grins) But I did enjoy saying it. Ma and Pa in, and I can tell by their faces that they don't like it. (Mum thinks it is dirty, 'Why don't you put on a nice suit and sing a nice song?' she says.) But Viv thinks I am brilliant and need not restrain Fagin at all – he can't be overdone because he is an uninhibited clown figure.*

I excuse myself to guests and sit behind the make-up screen. Look at FAGIN for a moment. Sigh a little.

FAGIN	(*peering back at MOODY through the mirror, and dabbing surgical spirit on his whiskers*) We did a good show, Ronny Boy, why you miz?
MOODY	(*carefully soaking the whiskers in a dish of spirit*) The applause! The folks say it came up big for Georgia, didn't go any more for me.
FAGIN	Don't worry, my dear. A little professional jealousy never 'urt anyone.
MOODY	(*wiping on removal creme with his hand*) Jealous? Of her! That yiddisha ham! I know, I know, I should talk! But I'm an old-fashioned ham, not a mess of Method mannerisms!
FAGIN	(*wiping his eyes, as they twinkle with mischief*)

Dodger and Oliver got more applause than both of yer!

MOODY   (*finishing off with Kleenex*) Wonderful! They deserve it! Clever kids! If I liked Nancy as much, I'd be cheering for her! If it was Vivienne getting the applause, I'd actually celebrate! And anyway, I gotta lotta leeway to make up in the next couple of weeks and I need the stimulus of competition. (*Thinks*) I'm astonished actually, because her performance is so overdone.

FAGIN   (*standing up and washing his face in the sink*) Well, I'm all done! You can go now! Hey! (*Pointing to his clothes*) 'Ang me up!

Looks like the old Enigma has taken on the trappings of a Paradox! For after the show, in the dressing-room and at the stage door, I am getting plenty of Personal Praise, but that same praise made public and measured in intensity of applause is no more than Georgia's!

It is petty, of course; it is what they call Show Business. And it meant that I was going to beaver away in the next couple of weeks prior to the West End, working on tape, dreaming up shtick, building the laughs, fixing the character, polishing the dialogue, making up all the leeway (my goodness, I haven't started yet) just so I could put that pettifogging Peruvian Princess in her place! If there has to be a fight, let it be a clean, straight fight, may the best man win! Come on, baby, light my fire!

And so the graft-with-audience began. The really hard work. Cutting out dead lines, filling every gap that cried out for a laugh, testing it with an audience, and, once found, setting that line in concrete. Another Paradox! The ultimate ad-libber, the ever-vigilant improviser, never changes a line once it is sanctified by a laugh. Or gets a bigger one. Or leads to another one. Or germinates a running gag. Ad-libbing is not a vain indulgence, it is a strict science. Karl Popper is never far away when there is testing to be done!

Which leads us to probably the most important part of any rehearsal, the tape work. Sooner or later on every show, as the lessons of rehearsal are pretty well absorbed, there comes the time to sit down and record every word of the script on tape, listening carefully not just for meaning and dramatic or comedic impact, but for diction and articulation, and, where final consonants are still lost, taking the seemingly artificial step of over-articulation.

Strangely enough, this was where I found and fixed Fagin's speaking voice. A cockney accent, with a soupçon of schmaltz and a piquant dressing of over-articulation . . . and perhaps a little test phrase, m'sieu, to tease the palate and be whispered to oneself just before one goes on, something like Fagin's opening line, meeting Oliver:

'I 'ope . . . I shall 'ave the honour . . . of your in-ti-mate ac-quain-tance.'

All that I could do on my own. But I also needed the invaluable input of others, however much I didn't want it.

Vivienne, fellow clown, strict repetiteur (no paraphrasing allowed!) and judge of a reading, knowing exactly where I was going, and usurping the director's control only because that is the prerogative of kindred spirits.

Getting notes from Bart at every performance that my voice was too husky (he was right), and I should sing *all* the lyrics not speak odd lines (tell that to Rex Harrison!). Much as I sympathised with the fact that he wrote the damned thing, I asked Peter to let me do my Fagin and not Lionel's.

Stage management finally giving me belated props, setting treasure box *exactly* as I want it, handkerchiefs on the line *exactly* as I peg them, props *exactly* in place and *exactly* right way up! And just to be sure, check them every show at the half! Explore, fix and polish, explore, fix and polish!

And finally, of course, the director, Peter Coe, who was not entirely popular with the cast because of his acerbic wit and a quite ruthless and justified determination to mould this show into a dramatic masterpiece, *his* way. After Wimbledon, the musical director was replaced with the great Marcus Dods, the only conductor who could keep his twelve-piece orchestra in step with a frenetic Fagin (who not only ad-libbed the words but the tempos and the crotchets) and stay smiling at the end! And the choreographer who walked out because Peter replaced the artifice of choreography with naturally moving groups, once again, as all great directors do, keeping the Truth in Dramatic Line all through.

As for me, although I sensed a general air of amused disapproval because Fagin was such a naughty actor, he generally let me go my own tragi-comic route, ranging from the terror and desperation at the threat of 'the drop', to the anarchic, continuously creative mischief that rippled (under my Tombackian influence) throughout my gang. He used to drop in large sheets of badly-typed notes, most of them about the technicalities of performance, including a tendency to become inaudible around the 'quick count-up', and leave too many pauses between lines. It was only on the last Friday of the Wimbledon try-out that he came into my dressing-room after the show and gave me the only note I ever needed for the rest of my career.

> *June 24th. I go in for notes. And afterwards Peter comes in and says I am losing the realities of the situation and seem to be trying to be funny. Viv is there and we both agree it is a valuable point and so tonight I THINK about everything I do to make it real and they all think it is much better, though to me it is dull and lacks the attack and zip of last night.*

Whatever I may have thought then, I have never forgotten that evening when Peter Coe virtually gave me carte blanche and said 'Do what you like, now make it real.' Something to write on your dressing-room mirror, eh?

'DO WHAT YOU LIKE, NOW MAKE IT REAL!'

Those words somehow knitted me together. Peter had put me into the driving seat with a controlling thought and the actor and the clown steered as one.

June 25th. *Go into Wimbledon for the last night. Peter says my performance last night was magnificent.*

And so the Wimbledon preview was over. We had had dead houses, good houses, hysterical houses, I had loved the times I won the evening, hated the times I drew! Didn't actually ever lose! But I still needed to know why I didn't win every time, that is, trump the competition with Personal and Public Praise, by solving at last the mystery of the Enigma and all that followed thereon.

12

The Enigma Turns Sour

Musical comedy became my consuming hobby during those inspirational student days at the London School of Economics, probably thanks to *Guys and Dolls* when it uplifted me to the gods the half dozen times I went to see it from the balcony of the London Coliseum. I loved the Runyonesqe paradox, the mix of vulgarity and class, the stilted dignity of the highly moral delinquents. Stanley Green, in *The World of Musical Comedy*, called them 'highminded lowlifes'. And I loved the story that Feuer and Martin, probably the greatest producing team in musical theatre, cancelled the Broadway opening of the show at the last minute because, quite simply, they didn't think it was *ready*! How much did that cost them? How many producers would have the sheer nerve to 'rock the boat'? And how many could bask in the glory of finally presenting, Feuer-and-Martin-shape, probably the greatest musical ever?

However, apart from that kind of courage, just imagine what went into getting it ready. Actually, that was the bit I loved best! What was most stimulating to me, the part I envied most about the creative process of that musical, was the long, protracted tour which was needed to knock the show into shape before opening on Broadway. How I envied that creative team, watching the show every night, (aaaaargh!) sitting through to the early hours in hotel rooms (yawn!) ordering salt beef on rye mit a pickle (burp!). How I wanted to be one of that privileged in-group of composer, librettist, lyricist, director, choreographer and producer, cutting and pasting and polishing and writing and rewriting, hour after hour after hour, week after week after week (yawn!) until they . . . thought . . . it was . . . ready.

Well, *Oliver!* was ready in two weeks! That's all we did at Wimbledon. The show, with its incredibly complex set, was de-choreographed, jigged a little, shifted round a little, barely cut, pasted, polished and rewritten, and not even in a hotel room mit salt beef und a pickle, because everybody lived in London. Most of the jigging and cutting was centred on the Bumble/Corney scenes in the Workhouse, a neatly controlled operation, as expected. But nobody expected the first night audience at Wimbledon to force the director's hand, with *Reviewing the Situation* opening the second Thieves' Kitchen scene and stopping the show cold so nobody could enter to carry on with the scene, and leaving me standing with, I have to say, very pleasurable egg on my face. Next night, *Reviewing* was moved to the end of the scene with sufficient space to work its wicked magic and to have me wheeled off on the set, with the applause continuing stubbornly (heh heh! excuse me!) in my absence.

As I said, I needed every minute of the two weeks to begin to get a respectable balance of laughter into the show (in fact, I didn't stop exploring lines and biz for six months), the mischief and fun settling in neat counterpoint to the panic and fear that summed up Fagin's world. And just to complicate things, the Enigma was sitting quietly, feet up on the conductor's lectern, basking in the footlights, waiting for each curtain call to stir things up.

Two short weeks! How was it done? And who could have

done it? Short of interviews with Albery, Coe or Bart, we might be allowed to hazard an informed guess that the Sean Kenny set, that magnificently organic, stage-busting structure, was not the sort of thing to take logistically, and certainly not economically, on any kind of budget-busting tour! So two weeks in Wimbledon-not-quite-in-London would have been Albery's strict limit. (To be followed, not many years later, by the economies of reduced-price, on-the-spot previews in town before opening.)

Then the incredible feat of restructuring a book-show within two weeks points to only one thing – that Coe and Bart had been 'getting the show ready' for some considerable time before (and the word is that Coe had a big say in the rewrite) so that the two weeks was sufficient to move the final pieces of the jigsaw into place.

Axiom: if you don't get the dramatic structure substantially right before you open, you'll never get it right.

This is not revue, after all, with interchangeable pieces, this is an integrated musical with a plot ideally driving through and binding dialogue and lyrics into one continuous, inevitable line of action!

There is no question that Bart hit the music and lyrics right on the button by avoiding the then current trend towards Bernstein's neo-classical pastiches, and going right back to his East End, cockney Jewish roots with a vernacular score that established him as England's foremost folk composer. And what of new numbers being written right through to rehearsal? Bart catching up on himself? Selling it unfinished? Or needing to work with his cast, writing it right once he knew who he was writing for!

All of this played a part in the masterly construct of so great a show in so short a time. But I suspect, apart from Albery's razor-sharp economic control and Bart's vibrant score, the true mastermind behind the swift restructure and instant success of *Oliver!* was Peter Coe. A classical theatre director who gave his work so powerful a dramatic spine, so well-considered a conceptual scheme, that it could (certainly at first) accommodate the heavy involvement of the zealous Method actress and the dangerous anarchy of the clown. A man who would not permit anything less than the Truth in Performance ('Make it real') and the Truth in Movement with no choreographed artifices, no classy but clichéd steps, but real people moving.

> *June 28th, 1960. Called early at Wyndhams' to polish 'Pick a Pocket' with the lovely Fiz* [Eleanor Fazan, principal dancer in the early revues] *who has replaced Malcolm Clare – he walked out in disgust when all his dance settings were altered and I don't blame him. But I do agree with the result that no conventional choreography has been used at all – it is the flow of groups on the mobile set that Peter has aimed at. Quite a ruthless bunch, this production team! But sound judges!*
>
> *Back to the theatre for more music calls . . . still there is an air of technical confidence about the whole show, stemming from Peter Coe, which makes all these preparations seem right. We open Thursday without a public Dress Rehearsal.* [At the New Theatre, to be renamed in 1973 in tribute to a great dynasty, the Albery.]

> *June 29th. This morning we do continuity, fixing the movement of the set and our links.* [First time I had been in a show where the set got more rehearsal than the cast. But of course it was the wisest policy. To watch the set moving round as the set pieces moved in, and the lighting changed, and the musical links melded it all together, and the actors entered right on cue, was nothing less than pure magic!]
>
> *I have been allocated a dresser who seems determined*

to be everywhere at once, but I suppose that will be OK. [His name was Harry and he was rather small, a sort of cross between Eric Blore, Hollywood's sniffiest butler, and Dickens's Uriah Heep, and former dresser to the great Larry Olivier, so maybe something would brush off!] *This evening we have our Dress Rehearsal and I get Viv in to watch – they have been going on at me to play smaller in this theatre but Viv says afterwards that I can be as big as I like. Fagin is Pan after all – and Pan cannot be cut down to size. The goat figure is a law unto itself and I must abide by that.*

June 30th. FIRST NIGHT, OLIVER! (NEW THEATRE) . . . and what a night! I don't think I've ever felt so relaxed and at home on stage. The show has a smash hit reception with 17 curtain calls, Lionel Bart makes a speech and I feel for him! Little Yiddle makes big time! And I have a great cheer at the end, establishing me, in all humility, as the star of the show. The dressing-room is crowded afterwards with friends, relatives – dear Ma and Pa and Aunty Rosie and Cis (Lou looking after baby) – and Rex Harrison comes in and it all adds up to the most exciting first night I have had yet. And I decide to round it off by taking Viv to the Mayfair Hotel for a quiet celebration – after all she is responsible for so much.

I have to say one more thing about that First Night and indeed the whole of the following year I was in the show. I have never known it before or since, though we had a few riveting First Nights even in the days of LSE. There was some kind of magnetomotive force in the air, a flux, a buzz, a charge; call it what you like, we moved around backstage in a force field that crackled and fizzed around us yet made no sound! It was more than excitement, it was more than the vibes that come with success, one might better believe it was the energy punched out towards us by the hysterical audiences who had managed to get tickets for the show and were already hyped up when they came in. I have always believed that actors on stage, however low their emotional state when they come to work, are charged up in the next couple of hours with energy generated by the assembled audience. They leave the theatre so high that if they don't go out to dinner or a club, they'll never be able to sleep. With *Oliver!* it was more than that – and the effect of the Enigma – as we will see later – was commensurately more than it might have been.

> *July 1st. Don't wait up for the papers but am in fact woken up this morning by an excited Ma who has bought the lot! The show has got raves and I have the best individual notices.*
>
> *At the theatre this evening I am tired after a restless day with little sleep . . . ah, well, I suppose one runs on one's own steam up to a point.*
>
> *Get card from Georgia, 'Congratulations, it was your night.' My, my, I am surprised.*

And I was actually touched to think there might be a softer side to Georgia. I had never chosen to be hostile towards and wary of her, I was merely reacting to the rough, tough insolence in her manner that made her so right for Nancy, but unfortunately alienated me. So maybe this would still be a happy show, we could all be friends, and the Enigma could lift its sticky hoof-prints off the footlights and take its negative effects elsewhere!

> *July 2nd. 3 o/c matinee. It is very hard work in this hot weather, encumbered with all my waistcoats and that enormous Harris Tweed gown, and that dresser who is beginning to make me jump. I can't turn around without*

finding him under my armpit. I've only got one costume all through, I don't even need a dresser, let alone a valet-butler-gofer-cum-bloody squire! But by the second house I feel fine with my man-for-all-trades elegantly serving drinks to Michael Redgrave who comes round after a resounding reception to congratulate me. I suppose this is the sign that one has, in a sense, 'arrived' – if the big stars come round. To see little old 'me!' And I suppose stars need a valet-butler-cum-bloody squire!

July 3rd. *I have a lovely Sunday press, singled out as the main performance. But one sticks in my craw – Ken Tynan's crit – a huge write-up of the show and some-where in the middle 'Ron Moody is an exemplary Fagin'.* [I don't know why I regarded that as a write-down, after all, in one line, however brief, it's the best thing he ever said about me. Maybe he was piqued because I went to LSE and he only went to Cambridge – or was it Oxford – one of those places]. *I am a little disappointed – I had hoped for more of a personal 'discovery'. But on reflection I know I shall never have that kind of review – I am a slow builder and seep into success not leap into it.* [As if it mattered! Who else in the whole world was sitting up in bed at that moment, swimming in newspapers and punching the air?]

Then get all my props and music ready for my début tomorrow at the Talk of the Town, the huge cabaret spot converted by Bernie Delfont from the London Hippodrome. Oh dear, four weeks to do, straight on top of the opening of Oliver! *I wish Sonny hadn't booked it but at least the Hippodrome is just over the road, and it isn't a late show. Who said 'Everything comes at once?' Four long weeks!*

July 4th. *In at 11.30 for band call at Talk of the Town*

. . . find Irene Hilda taking all day over hers . . . but she's a sweet lady so I wait patiently . . . and chat up the dancing girls, managing to avert my eyes from their overstretched rehearsal gear – well, it's only four weeks here! Dress rehearsal goes on and on and I really don't mind being here!

Do good show at the New but I am tired – then over for first night at Talk of the Town and find that I go down very well. But do 23 minutes. Robert Nesbitt comes round with Sonny and Viv, and is pleased but wants it tightened.

Matinee excellent today with all the pros in! Miriam [Karlin] thinks it fabulous, so does Miles Eason. Into Talk for re-setting act shorter, then back for second house. But I find suddenly that Georgia matches my applause. I must be going down a bit with fatigue. Well, at least it keeps me on my toes.

Cabaret fine with the shortened act, so now I can settle down there!

But I can't stop brooding. What if Georgia sent me that card to lull me into a false sense of security, thinking she has called a truce! Meanwhile, she does a Sylvester Stallone on me, sleeps till 2 pm, has a large steak lunch, works out in the gym for an hour, punches sides of salt beef, runs up the steps of St Paul's Cathedral and prances around like Rocky Balboa! Then she waits till Fagin has extended himself far too far doing cabaret, and she's in for the kill, left, right, left, right, left, right, KNOCKOUT!

I wake up with a jerk and have to think about the dancing girls to calm myself down!

July 8th. *Up late, to read the* Jewish Chronicle *rave for me as Fagin.* ['Something you'll be able to tell your grandchildren about' they say]. *Well, that's a relief!*

[Remember my considerable second thoughts about playing such an infamous character, and that, worst of all, Fagin was Jewish! And what would the *Jewish Chronicle* critic say about that?] *They say 'the brilliance of the interpreter is more than that of the writer.' I hope Lionel reads it.* [Although it doesn't say whether the 'writer' is Bart or Dickens. Either way, the JC backed me! I love to make my people proud!]

    Show fine tonight – a lot depends on the state of my voice – and so is Talk of the Town. I am beginning to like the cabaret very much.

July 9th. *Up late again today. I need lots of sleep with the double burden of* Oliver! *and cabaret, and the spur to effort that comes from Georgia's aggressive push every night. I am always lucky to have someone in every show who makes me work harder.* [I can't believe I wrote that!]

Harder and harder, because, as if that wasn't enough, I drove down to Bognor next day, on my Sunday off, to do three variety shows at Butlins! Wasn't that working a bit *too* hard? Hard? It didn't even occur to me! Nor did it occur to me that the rivalry with Georgia was no different from the clash of Tenor and Soprano in Grand Opera, the matching and re-matching of Primo Carnera and Max Schmelling in the ring, McEnroe and Borg at Wimbledon, arena after arena where for some reason the contenders all want to prove themselves best. And the jolly old Paradox takes a bow! For all the intensity of negative feeling between the rivals, ranging from dislike to hatred, the public love them both, win or lose, for they are the heroes that make the game worthwhile. Only in soccer is everybody allowed to hate *everybody*!

    And then fate steps in!

July 15th. *George* [the Company Manager] *rings to say* *that Georgia is off so I have to go in for rehearsal. Liz [the understudy] is very good as Nancy but I feel distracted – the applause at the end isn't good enough. Strange how I don't like Georgia but need her to spark me off in the show.*

July 16th. Second house excellent and Liz fine. Ma and Pa in and think it is marvellous so it shows it doesn't need Madame Brown at all. Go into Talk of the Town for a tear-up and really feel on top of the world – as a performer at any rate. Always makes me feel concerned when I start being pleased with myself.

July 17th. Sunday. Up early to be in for recording at Decca Studios [recording Oliver!] See Georgia who says she felt ghastly having to be off show. I feel sorry for her.
 Decide to go to the Talk of the Town party. Meet all the lasses and get on well with Jean Cragg, that lovely little blonde – have a veritable ball and am finally organised with a dancer. See her home to a large flat she shares with load of others [in Streatham], quite a community and I rather like 'em all.

Many years ago, when I was a student at LSE, I went to my first ballet at Covent Garden, sat way up in the amphitheatre and watched *Swan Lake*. Even at that distance, packed into that tilted egg-box of a seat, fearful of craning forward and going over the edge, my view of the *corps de ballet* swans, on pointe in their frilly tutus and white tights, absolutely devastated me. I had never seen anything so beautiful en masse. I vowed that thereafter all my girlfriends would be dancers and that one day I would marry one.

Jean Cragg was such a dancer! Classically trained in South Africa, she had come to England and become a specialty dancer in the Delfont and Grade extravaganzas. Petite and perfectly formed, she spoke with a slight Afrikaans accent and a very sharp tongue. Well, she seemed to like me, and I certainly liked her. Our friendship has lasted well over forty years and we are still in touch.

Why didn't I marry her? Why didn't I marry Vivienne? Because I was fated to marry much later and have six children (that's another book altogether!) and, apart from my work, those children are the prime and defining achievement of my material and spiritual existence. Which is a wordy way of saying 'nothing else matters', or, putting it into perspective, 'when a child is born, everything that came before had to be!' PS My wife, Therese, is a classical dancer. PPS She had to be, too!

Oliver! continued in tandem with the Talk of the Town.

August 1st. *I enjoy it as an aftershow item when I'm still hepped up.*

There was a terrific audience reaction in both theatres, and the feud with Georgia settled into a tolerable coexistence that still served the legitimate purpose of sparking off the scenes between us. She said to me once, 'Why can't we be friends?' and I said, 'Maybe the show needs it!' Maybe if I'd been a better actor, I could have simulated the dislike. But when I said the line 'Why Nancy, you're wonderful tonight! Such talent! Such an actrissssse!', hissing the final syllable with all the benevolence of a fork-tongued serpent, I couldn't have acted the crushing mockery of words spoken truly from the heart any more than I could have 'acted' the anger and terror when I threw Dodger across the 'Three Cripples' and Peter had to trick me to get mad! Now I felt that Georgia knew that I meant it, and I knew she added to the sting by taking it personally!

So at least *Oliver!* never settled down into a boring run. Along with a backstage rippling with that mysterious force, and the undercurrents of rivalry bubbling in the air, and plenty of the good old-fashioned vibes that come with success, we also had a pretty constant stream of film stars and fine actors coming back to pay their respects. I remember gazing upon the incomparable beauty of Vivien Leigh, who came backstage to visit me in what had been her old dressing-room during the celebrated Old Vic season, and actually asked me for a signed photograph!

Then there was the night Joan Collins came back with Warren Beatty and I couldn't find the words to let her know I was madly in love with her and how dare she marry Anthony Newley!

Another night Anton Dolin practically danced into the room, dressed with incredible elegance and élan, his fedora tilted to one side as if he'd just rolled straight in from the Riviera. Brillig sophistication, yet chatting away like a real pro. But none of the visits touched the night when the Great Man himself came backstage, ushered in by his former dresser, Harry.

> **August 13th.** *After the second show, as well as Frank and Mandy* [the Stygalls, two close friends from LSE]*, who should come in but SIR LAURENCE OLIVIER. What a nice man he is too – 'one of the lads' in his manner. Makes the evening for me and the others in the room.*

Frank and Mandy were thunderstruck, talked about it for years afterwards! The mighty Olivier, the greatest actor of his generation, not merely standing in my dressing-room, but chatting to me as an *equal*, as a fellow pro, about *my* performance! And oh, how I was dying to ask him how he felt when he gazed for a brief moment around Vivien Leigh's old dressing-room, what memories flooded into his mind about those wondrous days of the Old Vic! Happy times? Sad times? What does a room tell you when you come back for a brief visit? And what did we talk about? Well, a day or so earlier, I had had to visit Richard Blore, make-up adviser to Leichner, for advice on my eyes which had suddenly turned red and swollen and very sore. He said I had developed an allergy to eye make-up and couldn't use water-based or cream – so he suggested a wax pencil and little else. What rotten luck! I had to reduce my carefully-designed Fagin make-up to a niggardly wax pencil and felt awfully bare and under par on the very night that the great Olivier comes to see the show.

I tell him all this and he says my eyes, wax pencil or no wax pencil, are 'fascinating' and we chat about make-up and how one can reduce it after the character is established.

How about that? It makes you understand what it means to be 'a great man'. Oh, how I love this business!

As for Harry, the Little Man Always at the Elbow, at least he was telling the truth about dressing the Great One. And I had to admit, he did add a touch of distinction to an otherwise ordinary, scruffy backstage. He went with the comfortably superior furnishings in the top dressing-rooms, and made sure that I was always well stocked with all sorts of superior spirits. When I had visitors he provided them with drinks, stood attentively to the rear awaiting the next command, then took their glasses and washed them up. I didn't like it at first; I used to do all that myself and kept a better check on the booze. Except when John Regan or Dennis Price visited and knocked off a bottle of gin in one evening. Well, why not? It was a privilege to have them visit. When I was making up or resting, Harry stayed outside the door. I found out later that he used to shush anyone passing because the 'master' was resting, and it wasn't too long before he was ruling the roost in my name. I suppose I should have realised then that I was in a smash hit show, and, even though Albery never put my name above the title, had become a West End star.

But the West End is a small village. You can be much loved

in Fulham, but nobody knows you in Wigan. A West End star is like the mayor of a small village in the Himalayas. You've climbed to the top of the mountain, but people forget you're there.

And yet *Oliver!* was different. There was a steady stream of fan mail that I'm afraid I allowed to pile up, then had to spend a lot of time answering. There were the little gifts that people sent to thank me for a wonderful evening. I was really deeply touched. Somebody even sent me a stuffed snake from somewhere in the Far East! I opened the battered package with infinite care and when I saw it lying there in a nest of grass, I thought the bloody thing was alive and I'd offended the member of some insidious sect. I yelled 'Yach!' and would have thrown it across the room if I hadn't been paralysed with fright! I couldn't wait to unload it on some kinky member of the cast who liked that sort of thing. And then there were the special letters, the glowing tributes and thanks for the very special evening they had come to *Oliver!* to celebrate, such as birthdays or wedding anniversaries or, on Saturday nights, bar mitzvahs. And slowly it dawned on me, as all this warmth and affection flooded in, that something new was happening, that I was in this particular show not merely for the belly laughs and the kudos and the publicity and the notices and the money and the tax avoidance and all the other sublime artistic ends that normally motivate us, but to actually make people happy!

I'd made them laugh, yes! But that was because I *needed* to hear them laugh! The British psychologists will say it was a need for approval and American shrinks will say a need for love, and that may have been true when I was six, but since LSE I had been testing a system called 'deviation from the norm' or 'deviation from expectations', and laughter had become for me a matter of technique, a logical process, part of a scientific method. When Groucho plays Hamlet, he says to Ophelia: 'I am very proud, you follow me, revengeful, you follow me, ambitious, you follow me, well, stop following me, you make me nervous!' Was that an ad lib, straight off the top of the head? Nyah, that was a manufactured joke, straight off the 'sit-down-at-the-desk, work out the A-A-A-B of it' top of the head!

So this was more than getting laughs, it was an aura, an emotional thing, there was a lot of love and affection flying around, maybe that was where the magnetomotive force germinated. Maybe for the very first time in my career I was actually doing it for others, putting everything I had into making people happy! There was a lot of love in Lionel Bart's *Oliver!*

So why, why, *why*, did it all turn so nasty backstage? There's a Paradox and a half to pick over! The show that dispenses love out front, groans with hate out back! And let's not forget the Enigma stirring, ever so quietly – there it is, a flicker of malaise, ticking off the early warnings way up front . . . Albery refusing to give me fair dues of £150; his inflexible offer of £95 and year's get-out left a nasty taste . . . Georgia, a real tough cookie; I found it hard to warm to her . . . rehearse second Thieves' Kitchen, find to my horror Georgia doing the full hysterics! . . . second night at Wimbledon, applause comes up big for Georgia, doesn't get any bigger for me . . . awareness of competition drives me harder . . . first night at New Theatre I glow with confidence, have personal triumph! . . . yahaha! . . . open at Talk of the Town for four weeks . . . At the New, Georgia gets very strong applause, I must be going down a bit with fatigue . . . double show settles . . . Georgia pushes hard . . . Georgia loses voice . . . yahaha!

August 25th. Go in to see Martin, my dentist, and with his usual Yorkshire gall he says the show wasn't all that hot but wasn't Georgia marvellous – I don't think he is really a friend of mine at all.

August 31st. Oliver! *OK, but Judy Garland is in and Bart takes her in to see Georgia and not me – the little sod!*

September 3rd. Into Talk of the Town for last night which is excellent and full of new gags. Folks in with Auntie Rosie and I go round to see them before going to Irene Hilda's wrap party. See Jean Cragg home.

I was sad to finish at the Talk of the Town because cabaret has always been for me that unique point of theatrical contact where the act flourishes in total symbiosis with the audience. But not surprisingly, I immediately had more energy for *Oliver!*

September 17th. Second house, I go full out and am cheered at the end – old Brown is furious. Pfui!

There were one or two attempts at what the politicians like to call détente – but, alas, they didn't work . . .

September 8th. Show OK and invited over to Wyndham's after for Candide *party. Nice people but later I hear that Georgia took the mickey out of Dulcie Gray.*

September 9th. Am invited out after the show with Maxine Audley, Jill Bennett, Willis Hall and Lionel and Georgia to the White Elephant. Nice evening, but Lionel leaves early to avoid paying the bill – Georgia is so loud I can't believe it. So how can I be expected to like them?

Actually, I did like Lionel. I said rude things about him, as I said rude things in cabaret about everyone, vestiges of the old undergraduate predilection for the satirical crack and the topical jibe, our way of cutting the great big world down to size. And I really don't think he would have left early to avoid paying the bill, when he had a smash hit show and how many golden discs? And was so generous, entertaining at the mansion he bought in The Boltons, that he eventually went bust.

No, Lionel was a good boy. I just couldn't take Georgia.

October 1st. Do great in the last show and argue with Georgia. Pity.

October 6th. Georgia does all she can to kill my laughs; let her do what she likes. She can't win.

That's pretty well what we write in our diaries. The truth as it hits us at the instant of writing! And appropriate words to express it, although I confess to leaving out the choicer words here. (I was brought up in a swear-free house. In the RAF I would blue the air with the best, but in the home, not a syllable of vulgarity passed my lips.) At least I don't emulate Strindberg and Freud. They recorded everything. In depth. Low down dirty thoughts that shouldn't be read by a dog. Diaries are private, they are not meant to be read by a dog! Or a man! If a man picks up his wife's diary, or a wife picks up her husband's diary, or you pick up your best friend's diary, you all deserve everything you get. Especially if your best friend is friendly with your wife. So just don't pick up my diary! You might find yourself in it.

October 8th. Ronnie Cass in for second house – I do good show but Georgia very down and furious when I get my laughs – Ronnie doesn't like her at all, but he isn't alone in that.

October 10th. Show OK but Georgia goes berserk again [in performance, not off stage].

We've been running relatively peacefully now for just over three months, with no lack of Personal Praise so the Oxford Enigma must be patiently awaiting its moment. And the diary is giving us some Truth, the creative clown is giving us some Serendipity, and the whole damned thing is a Paradox! Stay with it! It gets better! Just don't pick up my diary!

November 3rd. Show OK, and Noel Coward comes round – he says my performance is still brilliant but seems harsher and over top. Nice man indeed. Margaret Leighton with him. [My gosh, what's up? A visit from theatre royalty to give me *notes*? A briefing from Bart's buddy, Coward, because Bart is banned from back-stage bitching?]

November 4th. While I am still worrying a little about what Noel could have meant, Sonny tells me there have been complaints about my performance – he heard it from Bart's agent – so? Who better?
Tonight, after show, Viv comes in – just when I needed her she was in, watching! How marvellous! [And so incredibly coincidental, Sonny!] *We check through the script and discover that I have been overdoing some of it – slowing down a lot until it had lost its zing.*

November 5th. Lionel asks me to come to lunch today and he gives me his notes which are all the same as Viv's last night. He has coffee, I pay the bill, the tightwad. [No, that's hardly fair, after all, he only had a coffee.]

November 8th. Second house OK, but I feel I have weakened and I don't know why. [Do we have another sniffy little Enigma to cope with here?]

November 14th. At show tonight, one of Dad's men in

[Dad was Head of Department at ABC] *so is Peter O'Toole, and I do a bad show. Talk it over with Viv and Rafael* [showbiz photographer] *and we think it may be the clown is missing, subdued by too many bosses.* [Easily done, losing the character as the show runs – that's why Robert Lewis had you keep the rehearsal script with all the notes!]

November 15th. At matinee and this evening, I try to bring back the mad old lip-licking Fagin – dear old Elias Tomback from Tottenham Shul is in and comes round with tears in his eyes. He is so proud. How marvellous. And I feel I am on to the answer at last.

November 16th. Tonight, I do an excellent lip-licking, eye-rolling, enjoying-himself Fagin – the old clown is back! [I had made the terrible mistake of playing it straight – and without mischief! Mischief! MISCHIEF!]

Minor Enigma resolved – character lost and found.

November 18th. Every night is excellent now, for Fagin is back!

November 22nd. Lionel Bart comes round after, raving mad because I am doing Fagin the old way – 'defying his notes'. I allow the bumptious little nit to stamp out after a few caustic remarks about his luck in choice of collaborators.

He still didn't accept an author's need for an actor's input, and his incredible good luck if the actor was also a creative writer who provided witty lines and inventive business free of charge or credit. He attacked my input but managed to keep it in.

November 23rd. Into New for talk with Peter Coe about Lionel Bart's stupidity and the burden that fell on Fagin to keep the show fresh.

My training in revue conditioned me to keep exploring the text for dead spots, and the prepared mind of a social scientist kept me alert for new business and gags for at least six months of the run. But working with children added another element – boredom! Fagin's Gang, for all their hyperactive energy in rehearsal, would be staring wide-eyed around the stage and totally uninvolved with the action by the end of the first week. I had to change business, lines, focus – picking on different boys each night – keeping them guessing – enhancing all this with a swift kick in the rear for any laddie staring blankly into space. I had been a teacher at Clark's College many years before, and failed completely to keep order – I sympathised too much with the boys and the boring old lessons. I had sessions within the category of Current Affairs where I let them all read their favourite comics. Always the odd man out.

But Fagin in charge of his gang was a whole new kettle of fish – this was my career, my profession, there was no way any of these boys could subvert my control for one split of a second that they were on my stage! Fagin's Kitchen was a *real* place and they lived in it for *real* and Fagin ruled them with an iron fist! So Moody's Mad Mischief wasn't quite as outrageously manic as it looked. A Clown was in charge and he had to have total, flexible, affable control.

December 3rd. Matinee fine but I have to slosh Dodger who occasionally goes over the top.

The 'slosh', or clip round the ear, or the sharp boot, is a necessary skill to be learnt in all its multiformity by those who deal with children, genus: actor; species: naughty; and it is rewarded by a look of shocked disbelief and a willingness thereafter to obey. And most important of all, that's it! No black looks or stored up grudges! They were boys! I loved 'em all!

December 16th. Go into theatre to find a stupid letter from Bart in which he takes four pages to tell me what an awful performer I am and how anti-Semitic many Americans feel I am as Fagin. What a bloody stupid little bastard.

A letter so full of bile tells you more about the writer than the recipient.

December 17th. Call at New for talk to Peter about Bart's fatuous letter – he suggests I ignore it – he [Bart] *had sent copies to Albery and Peter.* [I'm surprised he didn't set it to music.] *Am very pleased to receive this support and do good shows. Last night at the Savoy* [Hotel, in two weeks cabaret] *is very good and they ask me to come again.*

December 22nd. Show fine tonight with Paddy, Irving [Paddy Stone and Irving Davies, England's finest team of choreographers], *and Ernst* [Urbach]. *All think Bart is stark raving mad when I tell them about that letter. He'd better not come near me again.*

December 24th. Georgia, believe it or not, wants to make up and gives me a set of brushes – well, we'll try.

December 26th. Manage to keep Xmas spirit before going in to first of the dreadful matinees. [Donald Albery nearly had a strike on his hands when he unilaterally declared two shows a day over Xmas! As always, I took what I was given, and instead of a half-hearted walk-

through, went for the festive feel of it and worked harder.
Like the old army trick on route marches, step it out and
it's a piece of cake!] *Lo and behold, Vivien Leigh comes
round to see me* [her inexpressibly lovely face glowing!].

December 28th. *Call from Sonny to say Jock Jacobson,
Bart's agent, saw me perform on Boxing Day and is on
my side completely about the performances.*

Well, there's a lot of words that mean just that, but
'exoneration' will do. Over the years I've disagreed (as who
has not) with writers, directors and actors and, whilst
allowing for the instances in which I have been right,
whereby my viewpoint is happily proven, and those where I
have been wrong, whereby I have gratefully learnt, I have
generally taken the cherished audience, 'that lot out front', as
the final arbiter.

And to put all the backbiting, backstage gossip into
perspective, there was a great big world outside the theatrical
claustrophobia of *Oliver!* and I was deeply involved in it.
Cabaret week at the Savoy on a stage the size of an Olympic
swimming pool, learning to be big enough to handle it
. . . recording *Alice in Wonderland* for television with me as
the Mad Hatter (I wonder why?) . . . a selection from *Oliver!*
at Drury Lane for the special Xmas matinee in front of the
Queen Mother, with everyone backstage randy (or claiming to
be) because of a dancer and movie starlet called Imogen
Hassall, an incomparable beauty who performs a solo dance
with the wings packed tight with drooling actors (we keep the
gag running all through the evening show at the New) . . . and
all the time working on a new TV series for the BBC, with the
warm approval of Eric Maschwitz and Tom Sloan. And,
ornery as ever, it isn't the chance of television fame that
excites me, but the chance of writing it myself.

And a little human touch! I decided that 1960 has been a

very good year, and it's Xmas, and I want to make it special for the two finest women in my life.

December 23rd. Go out today to do more Xmas shopping and buy a couple of MINKS! [Stoles, not coats, 1960 wasn't that good!] *A silver blue for Mum, and a sapphire for Viv, who got hers first on Xmas Eve.*

December 24th. My greatest moment comes tonight, when I get rid of Harry, so that Viv and I are alone and I can give her the mink . . . she doesn't believe it at first, then cries. She is transported! We go to the White Elephant, have a lovely meal while Viv shows off her mink and we're given presents by the boss [dear friend and restaurateur, Victor Brusa] *and stay on to watch the waiters play roulette.*

December 25th. Mum liked her mink in a quieter way, partly because she didn't know what it was. [She opens the swish, fancy West End packaging and looks at the contents. 'What's that, rabbit?' she says. I explain the rarity of the creatures that provided the elegant fur and she nods and puts it back in the box and puts the box away in the wardrobe and seems to put it out of her mind. But she wore it many times over the years, notably at the World Premiere of the film of *Oliver!* at the Odeon, Leicester Square, nine years later, and when she did she looked radiant.]

Seeing how lovely they both looked in their furs, I think I may have had the best of the deal, enjoying the company of two women to whom I gave special presents and who gave forth a special light.

January 1st, 1961. And so we are off on the New Year,

the next decade, the New Thirties perhaps? Will it be a time for romantic revivals?

January 24th. Just before I go in to matinee I receive innocent call from Brenda Houston who works on the Mirror asking me about the likelihood of my going to Broadway and if I would play Fagin any differently. Apparently they have heard all about Bart's letter – later at theatre, Ann Jenkins [Albery's assistant] *comes in and says some awful item is being printed tomorrow, and after the second show, Sonny comes in and says the lawyers have averted a crisis. After all this dramatic hoo-hah, I ring Brenda again and she says they have squashed the story and didn't know what all the fuss was about. I'll bet Bart wishes he never wrote that stupid letter anyway.*

And who had access to the letter and who could possibly have told the Press about it?

January 26th. Another good house tonight and I find I now work consistently according to my little formula.

After so many ups and downs sustaining the character of Fagin, incurring the wrath of Bart, and needing Vivienne's remarkable insight plus the annotated rehearsal script to remind me of its essentials (eternal thanks, oh, mighty Robert Lewis for your inspired guidance), I tried to simplify, to codify the key qualities of 'the old goat' in a small mantra-like couplet, to be chanted at key moments:

> 'Eyes bright, voice light
> For Pan is on the stage tonight!

And from that, muttered under my breath, I would take

heart and direction – eyes bright with mischief and unpredictability, voice light and flexible, never hoarse or harsh, and dear old Pan, the essence of the Great Charlie, Grimaldi, Deburau, filling the heart, the stage, the theatre, with the happy panacea of laughter!

January 28th. Second house very good, but doesn't seem especially different until end when I get an enormous cheer on my call.

January 29th. Settle down today to finish the 'Musketeer' TV script . . . in the two weeks at the Colony I should have six acts ready for testing, all at about six minutes each.

The Marx Brothers did it first, took a show on the road and knocked it into shape before filming it. Now I was about to write, test and break in six routines in cabaret, prior to their use in a series of six television shows. The series was, if nothing else, an original concept, based on Weber's three kinds of power, i.e. Force, Domination and Manipulation. (Oh, Moody, you cerebral swine, can't you do something simple? But what is more simple, more complete, replies the cerebral swine, than an exhaustive breakdown of the ability to act, viz, energy manifested in control, ergo, Power?) I had this insignificant common man (Moody) entering various types of institution (A Clock Factory, Tin Pan Alley, A Big Store, etc.) and there meeting the Bully (Force), the Boss (Domination), and the Fixer (Manipulation) who variously influence his journey into, through and off the premises, having by this time forgotten what he came in for. Its relevance here is simply that it was taking up every inch of my spare time, leaving me little room to worry about the backstage machinations of *Oliver!*

January 31st. Second house very nice and I get cheered at end – maybe I have got the character right now.

February 7th. Up late, not completely refreshed to find an obnoxious quote by David Merrick, the USA impresario who is putting on Oliver! *He says it will be a smash on Broadway and due to Bart – he doesn't need any of the cast because actors are unimportant. So much for his judgement . . . I find that the atmosphere at the theatre is almost unbearably oppressive with all the talk of Merrick and Broadway, and the sight of Bart, dressed like a black gnome, sitting on the stairs.*

February 10th. Have the great pleasure of turning down an invitation to lunch with Donald Albery – I don't want hospitality, and any business he can discuss in normal hours. [Buying me lunch? With food? He must want something pretty badly!]

February 23rd. Call from Sonny to say that he has contacted Albery (fool!) and if I stay on with Oliver! *at rise in salary, I can go to USA with the show in 1962! BIG DEAL! I will go in to discuss terms with Sonny tomorrow, but I wouldn't dream of tying myself to one show for so long!* [No ego here, just the wisdom of staying loose for the offers buzzing around the sublime success of *Oliver*! Who knows, the fabulous firmament of films might open any moment! So is it Hurrah for Hollywood, and a young boy's dreams, or another grim year of Albery, Bart and Brown?] *Show fine tonight. Take American friends to the White Elephant and have nice evening, marred only by the sight of Georgia, dressed in dirty purples and blacks.* [Oh, Moody, Moody, you really don't like that girl! Not without reason, perhaps. But as my mother puts it, 'Be kind Ronnie.']

February 24th. *go in to Kavanagh's and tell Sonny what I want – exclusive top billing* [a blessing for those who do not suffer fools gladly] *. . . £400 a week* [Too-shay, Albery, for the measly £85?] *. . . and house seats – for a limited period* [to save that awful hassle with the Box Office] *. . . or I leave the show. Now we wait.*

March 7th. *As if it wasn't bad enough last Saturday, when Georgia went into a frenzy because I got a laugh, she goes mad again tonight. Well, Fagin is a mischievous old goat and I'm just doing my job, what does she expect?*

There's no question that her heavy method acting is so damned se-ri-ous – so much more than a bit over the top – that it's always on the edge, one might say, of risibility – and the more intense the scene, the bigger the release of laughter. But I'm not mocking it or her, merely exploring Fagin's terrain for nice pickings. And serendipity has not yet had its day – there are, legitimately, laughs yet to come!

March 8th. *I am heartily fed up with all the ticket requests – I have now ordered a dozen or so and have to ring around for those that wanted them.* [What am I, a ticket agency?] *Good house and I play very kindly to Georgia, which infuriates her even more.* [Incredible that this East End cookie really thinks I'm mocking her, and not her character. Fagin mocks everybody, even daring to jibe at Bill Sykes, but if Georgia is taking it personally, what is Fagin supposed to do, send her flowers? Ayayay!]

March 9th. *Show OK and Madame has shouted herself out so we have peace tonight.*

March 13th. *Sonny finally tells me about Albery. He will pay 5% if I will stay on for a year and go to America.*

Won't do top billing above title because he wants to sell the show not me – as I suspected. I know if I did the full deal I would get all I wanted but we shall see.

March 14th. *Show OK . . . and on to the Colony with Eric and Viv for the first night. And it is fine.* [For the next two weeks, in addition to eight shows of *Oliver!* and occasional charity lunches, I spend my days polishing the six television scripts for my first series, so that items from them may be tested in the cabaret at the Colony. The reaction is excellent and the numbers, substantially, work. But there are repercussions.]

March 15th. *Into theatre to find Peter Coe champing at the bit and saying I was dreadful yesterday and embarrassed the audience – what claptrap! I was tired but I did keep up the fun – which is what counts. But I have to leave out the handshaking bit which leaves an awful gap – the show is duller tonight too. And I keep swallowing my moustache.* [But I always listened to Coe. From the very first rehearsals in Wimbledon, I realised that his acerbic crackers always concealed a choice little gift! He floated concepts, sensed something was wrong, couldn't always pin it down, but together we solved it. On stage, I think I did my best work with him. I miss him very much.]

March 16th. *Coe calls in to ask why I didn't come in for rehearsal.* [With all I'm doing, little wonder I forgot.] *I tell him of idea for making the handshaking real – so we put it back in and it makes all the difference. Good show.*

March 17th. *Singing lesson, and in, a little late, but no niggle, for rehearsal with Peter. It is very useful and no arguments, tho' a little tension especially when Black-*

eyed Brown comes in – oh, I do hate that ——. [Moody! Be nice! And hope you never read *her* diary!] *Good clean show tonight and big reception at the end so it looks as if Peter's call has had some benefit.*

March 20th*. Viv goes round front to see show and thinks I have lost the mischief due to Coe's restriction. I am a bit fed up at this but I realise it is right.* [Whatever you do as a comedian, Pan has to be on that stage! Get all the truth you may into it, make it as real as you can, but never lose that incandescent light of mischief, that very soul of a comedy performance. I suppose what I needed was a Peter Coe to keep me real and a Vivienne Martin to keep me naughty. In those days, I was blessed with both, driving me back and forth like a tragicomic ping-pong ball!]

March 22nd*. Call today for Peter Coe to clean up show – I find his calculating rudeness too much now* [actually, the rudeness is no worse than it's always been] *and tell him that these alterations are his opinion against mine – if he wants somebody else he can get him now – so he says he will. Good. Am furious all the evening and do such a fierce show that I get that special applause at the end.*

Oh, dear, first Albery, then Georgia blows her top every time I add a laugh, Bart sends me a four-page diatribe that accuses me of alienating America, and finally, Peter Coe, whose caustic comments have till now bounced off the armour of our mutual respect, has joined the club. Heaven save us from paranoia and a full-frontal persecution complex but I don't think my colleagues share the public's affection for Fagin! And here am I, Stanley, threatening to walk out, and here is he, Ollie, threatening to accept! As if we mean it! It's the success of *Oliver!*, it's *The Treasure of Sierra Madre*, it's the power of gold to turn a man's mind, and the power of success is not far behind. We've all been bitten by the bug!

13

The One-Sided Feud

April 6th. *THE FEUD – NIGHT ONE. At theatre this evening for no reason known to me, Madame Brown suddenly goes mad during 'I'd Do Anything' and begins to play up all through the scene – I have been joking with Keith [playing Oliver] – she seems to think it's aimed at her – but this is quite inexcusable. George comes round and asks why the feud has broken out again – I say I am at a loss. She is just mad or got some bee in her bonnet.*

I am stunned. Not so much by Madame Brown getting a touch of spring fever for no apparent reason but by George Rowbottom, Company Manager and loyal collaborator from past shows, asking *me* 'why the feud has broken out again'. Again? There hasn't been a feud *before*! A strained relationship maybe, a mutual dislike which we made little attempt to conceal, but no life-or-death struggle, no recall of ambassadors. So why does George try to drag old, innocent *me* into this peculiar outbreak by new, frisky Nancy? Bribery? Sex? (You have to know George to realise how funny that is.)

April 7th. *Things bubble up today. Sonny rings to say*

Albery called him about last night, and if the 'feud' does not stop he will call the Theatre Council. What has that to do with me – she suddenly went berserk, not me.

Ohmygosh, now Albery's aboard the good ship Humbug! What brought him in? Bribery? Sex? (Do not laugh, this is serious!)

April 7th *(continued). THE FEUD – NIGHT TWO. After singing lesson, into theatre to find her still playing up and hostile – and am furious when George comes round to read me the report he sent in on last night's affair, saying the 'feud has broken out again to the detriment of the show'. I accuse him of being weak and afraid because this is the only reason he could have implicated me in something which was her fault. I find it difficult to believe that my old friend George could have done this to me – but is he so weak he crumbles at the first test? I insist he keep close watch on her movements to kill my laughs. What a business – is it a coincidence that it comes just as I am preparing my TV?*

Well, at least we're back on line with an unbelievable Paradox – a show that sends off its audience with songs in their hearts, sends home its cast with lead in its belly! And we even have a rip-roaring Enigma – what's got into her? – what half-truths is she dreaming up for her cronies at the Buckstone Club, what awful things does she say about me over a double gin at Ronnie Scott's?

I go into Peter's the Barbers in one of the elegant Arcades that link Piccadilly and Jermyn Street, and there, by an incredible coincidence, sitting in the next tonsorial chair to me, is the formidable Sam Wanamaker, aesthete, artiste, powerful actor and director, theatre designer, inspiration for the multi-layered Shakespeare Theatre in Liverpool, future father of the New Globe on Bankside, and friend of Georgia Brown. So I suppose it is inevitable that her name should sooner or later pop up in our conversation, with the neat theatrical touch of two half-hearing hairdressers snipping away around us, proving how far the winged dart of gossip may travel, with 'Chinese Whispers' leading to the inevitable distortion of its message. But Sam is not that kind of pro, here is a substantial intellect sniffing out the truth and in some way attempting to bring peace to our troubled waters because he likes us both. 'Georgia is upset,' he says, 'because you aim to get laughs in her dramatic scenes. She is a Method actress who is deeply immersed in her character, entirely lives as that character when she is on, and the clowning and laughter which you bring in are breaking her concentration.' 'Absolutely,' I agree. 'But the tragi-comedian handles both sides of the coin. And if she is so deeply immersed in her character, why does she try to kill my laughs?'

Sam nodded and went back to contemplating his haircut.

April 8th. THE FEUD, NIGHT THREE. The fun and games continue with Mata Hari, both shows, and I ring George to make sure he is keeping watch. I am quite furious at being implicated like this – I am a clown who improvises and it is obvious this witch resents my freedom and is fighting me by trying to kill my laughs – what an atmosphere. But I don't do anything to worsen the situation – except fall backwards off the stool – not really the sort of comedy I want, but what a laugh! I shouldn't do it, I know – I should keep a clean slate to justify my plea. What a bloody business – and nothing is being done to stop her. Receive letter from Albery asking me to sustain quality of show by abstaining from fight – what about her still doing it then?

Many years later when Sam Wanamaker had built a huge

tented theatre on Bankside in a substantial move towards the reconstruction of the Globe, I played Polonius and the Grave-digger – interesting double – to Keith Michell's *Hamlet*. It was not an easy ride, because Peter Coe, disciple of Jan Kott, the influential Polish critic and writer, had Elsinore updated into a Fascist state; and Polonius, written as an old fool and usually played so, did not fit into this autocratic mould. This was one tough Enigma! In the struggles that followed to solve it, Coe became so abusive and personal, even threatening to replace me, that I went in to see Sam and tell him I would have to leave because I expected help and respect from my director, not this cold-blooded, unjustified public abuse. Sam was instantly one hundred percent on my side. He begged me not to leave, insisted this production needed what I could bring to it, and had a quiet word with Coe. The sniping stopped, I found the character with Vivienne's sympathetic help in one of our lateral thinking sessions, playing Polonius as Goebbels with dossiers on everybody, and *Hamlet* went on to a formidable success with quite a few notices for me that justified Sam's confidence. 'The actor of the evening,' said Felix Barker in the *News*. Even Milton Shulman in the *Standard* praised my prototypal achievement, albeit by 'trampling roughshod over the lines'. And Sam Wanamaker proved that he was not only a great Manager but a great man who could make definitive sense of Polonius's words to his son, Laertes:

> *Those friends thou hast, and their adoption tried,*
> *Grapple them unto thy soul with hoops of steel.*

How could you compare the values of a mensch with the mendacious and unfair letter sent to me by Albery?

April 9th*. Sunday. Go for a drive to Brighton with the folks, but the day is marred . . . I am deeply hurt by the* *injustice of this official action taken through George by Albery. I decide I must write a letter to Albery telling him the whole story in detail.*

April 10th. See Albert Locke about the Palladium show next Sunday . . . find them all so nice and co-operative and he is so helpful . . . I wonder why I even bothered to think about that stupid woman.

April 10th (continued). THE FEUD, NIGHT FOUR. This evening, she cuts the hanky gag by putting it back into her bosom instead of allowing me to flit in, grab it, and hang it on the line. I must write that letter to Albery because this behaviour is inexcusable.

April 11th. THE FEUD, NIGHT FIVE. All Madame's efforts fail today so it seems that justice will prevail through her inadequacy.

April 12th. Go mad and order a new Vortexion Tape Recorder from Wood Green, and a new Zodiac Convertible from RK Motors. Well, well, that ain't bad spending for one day, is it?

April 12th (continued). THE FEUD, NIGHT SIX. Show unfortunately very messy tonight and my good humour quickly dissipates and have another row with old gutless Rowbotham who seems to have switched his allegiance right over to Georgia. My goodness, is this what Show Business does to people? I finish the letter to Albery, stating the whole case and leave it at Stage Door – now see what happens.

April 13th. THE FEUD, NIGHT SEVEN. Show tonight fine – I am so indifferent to all this stupidity that I cut the fall from the stool – I don't want that kind of laugh anyway. 'Funny Girl' can have it!

April 14th. *THE FEUD, NIGHT EIGHT. Into the theatre to find after show that Albery has sent me a letter to say he cannot do anything and Peter Coe refuses to call rehearsal because he feels it will be useless. Suggests I meet Brown over a cup of coffee. Right! They won't interfere. Then I know what to do tomorrow.*

This bizarre, one-woman 'Feud' has lasted *eight nights*! I have no idea what provoked the initial outburst, but the injustice of blaming me for it is infuriating, the refusal by any of the production team to intervene, pretty clear evidence of some kind of tacit conspiracy. It may well be that my success in building and empowering Fagin has aroused so much hostility that Georgia's defection has sent a ripple of *schadenfreude* through their miserable guts. The ingrates do not recognise how much energy and invention – so welcomed by the public – I have been putting into the show for their benefit as much as mine. And if they think that it is acceptable to sit back and let Georgia give me what they doubtless see as 'a taste of my own medicine', then perhaps they are suffering from more than a little envy at the huge cheer I get at the end of the show! Do we have here possibly too much Personal Praise? The Enigma in Reverse?

Well, we've already had the 'Oliversion' of *The Treasure of Sierra Madre*, the lust for gold corrupting the dedicated soul, now it's time for *Cat Ballou* with Lee Marvin, the miserable scarecrow of a drunk, going through a hilarious ritual cleansing before dressing up in the immaculate black and diamanté apparel of the highly-vengeful fastest gun in the West! And why not throw in a touch of *High Noon*, with Gary Cooper going it alone against the merciless killers, unsupported by the pusillanimous townsfolk! *Home Alone,*

Robinson Crusoe, Mr Smith Goes to Washington, one of the favourite themes of the world of entertainment, and now we have it here in mundane Maiden Lane – *Fagin Fights Back*!

Saturday, April 15th. *THE FEUD, NIGHT NINE. Feel very on top and ready to do my job today . . .*

Go in through the Stage Doors, swinging them shut behind me. The stage doorman sees me, gulps and ducks down into his cubby-hole, my feet clang and echo along the concrete passage, heads appear fast at dressing-room doors and disappear double-fast inside! Down the steps, turn right at the bottom, push open the door of Dressing-Room Number One, eyes flick around, casing the joint. Harry, somehow even smaller today, appears from the self-contained washroom, senses the mood, says nothing, begins to lay out the Fagin costume with the same pride as he once laid out Richard III for Laurence Olivier. White unravelling T-shirt; grey shirt with tattered collar; torn red neckerchief; patched-up hose; rough tweed knee-breeches; first long waistcoat with yellow braid; second red waistcoat with ornate, scuffed trim; third waistcoat open at front; long, orange-ish, triangular wrap; black, flat-topped, cardinal-type hat; and last of all, the inspirational touches, the anachronistic, mediaeval Pied Piper slippers that have steps of their own, and the finger-dancing, hand-tracing, eye-striking, ripped brown mittens that give Fagin's fingers a life of their own.

I wash my face and pat it dry, put on the tatty T-shirt, sit at the brightly-lit make-up table and stare into my own eyes for a long moment. I mutter and cackle a bit. Harry moves quickly away to the door. Moisturizer base, brown stick then brown liner to give the face its deeper shades and dirty spots, black liner to bring out the eyes and double their size, out with the tin of Clown White, the mask of the Clown, apply it with fingers, wipe it into place as Moody begins to disappear.

Apply the spirit gum to the chin piece, as little as possible –
filthy, sticky stuff for a sunny April morning – press on with
a damp towel, same with the moustache, press on with the
damp cloth, glue the sideboards, wig off the block, carefully
in place. Moody is gone, Fagin is sitting opposite calmly
surveying me from the mirror. What is the old goat thinking?
I suspect he is thinking: 'If you prick us, do we not bleed? If
you tickle us do we not laugh? If you poison us, do we not
die? And if you wrong us, shall we not revenge?'

I walk to the door, calm and in control, Harry opens the
door, averting his eyes, I walk up the stairs, pass through the
doors to the stage, the music of *High Noon* begins its sonorous
beat, I am in the wings, I check my personal props, step onto
the Kitchen revolve and begin to move in . . .

> **Saturday, April 15th**, (*continued*). *At the matinee I go to
> town on her – yet I do it all by business and all in
> character, never showing the audience what I am doing.
> I feel so much better I almost lose my urge, but though
> easier in the second house, I wait till she repeats the fall
> before my line and go to town on her again.*

It is a fascinating exercise in improvisation. She is
bludgeoning her way through the show, mainly distracting
and behaving like a naughty child who wants to get attention.
But I am perched like a kestrel on Sean Kenny's set, swooping
in with lines and business that feed off her clumsy tactics,
changing the timing of my lines so she can't pick her spot to
fall or laugh or move in her childish attempts to kill them.

But the pièce de résistance, the nonpareil, the crème de la
crème of the two-part feud that is now being enacted before
the ironically privileged audience, viewing a piece of theatre
history, comes amidst the uneasy excesses of the second
Thieves' Kitchen. This has always been my least favourite
scene, used by Georgia to flaunt the self-indulgent

mannerisms of the Method, and it has always been thereby on the edge of satire, screaming to be sent up. So it is not surprising that, half-formed in my mind, is the quintessential mock of the scene, indeed, of the entire relationship of Bill and Nancy. In his unlovely glower, she clearly sees the look of love, a backhander down the pub stairs has her singing *As Long As He Needs Me*, and a swift upper-cut in the Thieves' Kitchen just has to be some kind of foreplay. So I can hardly be blamed when I enter the scene, see her on the dirty, unscrubbed floorboards, well established as her favourite place – and say:

'What, is she on the floor again?'

The laugh went on! And on! And *on*! It was a *belter*! I never expected such a laugh, in fact, as with all new lines it might have got nothing. But it hit the jackpot. Well, in retrospect, think of the context. The brutalisation of Nancy is quirkily blessed with her adulation. She is motivated by some kind of masochistic mood-warp. An audience, observing this trend, already half-wondering how she can love a man who beats her for breakfast, will respond to the opening of that door, grateful that somebody has touched the secret spring, allowed them to recognise by the release of communal laughter what's been half bugging them all evening. She is indeed on the floor again! And what's this? Nancy crying? Floods of tears and a swift exit? Is she so deeply moved by Oliver's plight? Poor girl! Well, you can't expect the audience to know that she wasn't crying for Oliver Twist, not even for Nancy, but for Georgia Brown! You can't expect them to know she has just been given a lesson in good manners by the old man with the beard, who would much have preferred a happy show, reflecting the happiness of the audience, instead of this ugly episode of theatrical chicanery.

Saturday, April 15th *(continued). At the end of the show, I am cheered!*

And yet the triumph was qualified, often the case when the winner doesn't really need the victory, and can be generous to the other side. And it wasn't Georgia alone who made me mad, after all she was only taking a leaf from my book, improvising to make some kind of point that nobody, to my knowledge, actually established. If we had been friends, I would have enjoyed such a challenge, tragicomic acting is a highly communal trade, as in the revues, requiring wit, a well-trained funny-bone, a back-up of gags, a large helping of resource and a good deal of interaction. But we were not friends. So why did Georgia suddenly blow her top?

I believe it could have started on March 23rd, about three weeks earlier, when Peter Coe had a call on the Second Thieves' Kitchen and told Georgia to attack Sykes verbally, not physically. As a result Fagin's laugh came back on 'Why Nancy, you're wonderful today! Such talent, such an actrissssse!' But what if Georgia had wanted to stop that laugh and found the attack on Bill helped? Wouldn't she get pretty mad if Peter inadvertently cramped her little game? And might not that resentment have built up to the vengeful outburst and the Feud? Who knows, who cares?

April 17th. *Go in to see Albery who asked to see me – at last something will be done. But to my horror there is a little chap from the Theatre Council present – obviously a threat in case I refuse to co-operate. I had already decided to leave off the attack, but this threat is the last straw. I agree to a rehearsal with Peter – so I have got results after all – and that should settle this whole crazy business. But this is the first time my name has been smeared like this! Meanwhile, she is as wild as ever tonight.*

April 18th. Call with Peter and the Wolf. He legislates what is in and isn't in of all this mess, and it works out pretty well OK except that he uses the chance to stop me doing the things he doesn't like. I treat the whole thing flippantly whilst Madame is in tears the whole time – indeed for a while I actually feel sorry for her and the whole shabby affair.

Whether or not she learnt anything I had no idea. Especially when she came on stage for rehearsal and suddenly blurted out, in front of the whole cast: 'When I'm on stage, nobody looks at anyone else!' Maybe she found that in a copy of *How to Win Friends and Influence People* but I wouldn't guarantee it. It does, however, set me wondering all these years later whether there wasn't a frightened kid beneath that angry mask, and she wasn't behaving badly, she just didn't know how.

Is it guilt which has me thinking about Georgia? Why couldn't we get on? Why didn't the show give us the happiness it gave to the audiences? Who was to blame? Her, me, both of us? Could it be simply that we came from different backgrounds, the neurotic from the claustrophobic school of Method Acting, and the anarchist from the wide open world of Creative Comedy? I tried to sum up the difference in a few words:

> For the Neurotic Actor the stage is a prison
> For the Anarchic Clown the stage is a playground.
> And never the twain shall meet.

April 18th (continued). Anyway, the matinee and evening shows are peaceful and I am much happier because all this anger and stress that I have been feeling are only wasting my energies – and I need them all for the TV series. So it is good – and I am cleansed.

14

Peace

And it was indeed a good thing that unfortunate 'Feud' was resolved in time, because from that moment on I plunged into the six-part television series that I'd been writing over the last few months. What with filming by day and playing the last two months of *Oliver!* by night, I was about to take on the heaviest work load I had so far encountered. *Oliver!* settled down at last into a peaceful show, and without stress it could almost run (as Walter Matthau, American hilariton, might risibly have put it) on empty. But as Jimmy Gilbert (the TV Director) never ceased to warn me, a weekly TV series was pure hell. Ah, yes, maybe, but very well paid.

So I served my final months in *Oliver!* at peace! It never ceased to have the audiences cheering; it never lost its power to generate waves of affection over the footlights in both directions. And yet! Here we go again! Something was oddly missing.

April 20th. Go in for show which is very dull, needs all that spark, even of enmity, to lift some of the scenes.

May 2nd. Hear that Carol Reed was in – I shall never forget his prediction about me – I shall be a great comedian, he said.

June 1st. Into theatre to find Georgia off again which is always nice of her. Do a very good show and folks in – also, Albery comes round and congratulates me on the best performance I have done yet! Well, well, what is up his sleeve? He has obviously received the notice and wants me to stay on.

I had never been able to warm to Donald 'Economic Man' Albery, but I think he just couldn't handle people. He underpaid me, joined in a conspiracy to have *me* blamed for Georgia's painfully unprofessional outburst, threatened blameless *me* with action by the Theatre Council, and then expected me to stay on in this miserable show on *his* terms! Nyah!

June 26th. Into theatre for my last week in Oliver! *– one minute I'm up to my ears and next I shall be without any work at all.*

July 1st. And so to my last day in Oliver! *And I am not looking forward to it at all because I hate emotion and partings – I would just like to be out of it and that's that! The matinee is fine and a few friends look in – and surprise, surprise! Albery, his wife* [how could that chill-zone have married such a lovely lady?] *and Anne Jenkins come in to present me with a solid, silver tray: 'To Ron, our most excellent Fagin'. Well, well, I almost feel warm towards the man – but when I think how much pain he has caused me, I don't.*
    The second house is quite terrific! I have sustained

applause on my entrance, and at the end an enormous personal ovation and great cheers – just like the student days at LSE. Make a brief speech: 'It's 'ot, ain't it?' and have some drinks in the dressing-room which is overcrowded with cast and audience, with one or two happy exceptions, and some tears. And so it's 'Farewell, Oliver!' Farewell!

I slip away from the mob into private make-up for a few minutes, because I still have to change. Dump my heavy gear onto a chair, and as I sit in my torn T-shirt at the table, Fagin appears on the other side of the mirror.

FAGIN   Some speech! (*Relishing the words*) 'It's 'ot, ain't it?', 'e says. You're a card, ain't you? You . . . are . . . a . . . card!'

MOODY   I couldn't think of anything else to say.

FAGIN   It was perfect, my dear. The applause said it all! (*He wipes his make-up off on his side of the mirror*) Well, son, you sorry it's over? You gonna miss me?

MOODY   I'm gonna miss those wonderful audiences. I'm gonna miss my lovely boys. And most of all . . . I'm gonna miss you.

FAGIN   (*cackles and stops abruptly*) Well, why are you leaving?

MOODY   (*shaking his head*) Couldn't stand all that . . . (*He shakes his hand*) There's happier things ahead.

FAGIN   That why you don't want to go to Broadway?

MOODY   Partly.

FAGIN   (*musing*) Lionel should have supported you. He always supported me. There's absolutely nothing I wouldn't do for him. (*Thinks*) There's absolutely nothing he wouldn't do for me. In fact, we spent most of our lives doing absolutely nothing for each other!

FAGIN *and* MOODY *fall about.*

FAGIN I got that joke at a wedding – the best man told it.

MOODY You went to a wedding? I'm surprised they let you in. Do they count the presents afterwards?

(HARRY *knocks on the door.*)

HARRY (*nervously*) You alright in there, sir? You're laughing a lot.

MOODY It's OK, I just told myself a joke. Well, time to go. Good luck you old crook, it's been great!

FAGIN (*fading into the mirror as* MOODY *exits through the door*) Yes, sir, it's been great.

MOODY Farewell, Fagin.

FAGIN Farewell, dear boy.

Viv and Harry help me to load up an inordinate amount of fixed assets but not liquid (I leave the drinks and rented glasses with Harry), various goods and chattels including a complete set of Dickens (sixteen leather-bound volumes given to me by Viv on the first night a year ago and still not read because my nightly read was always the script of *Oliver!*), and more trappings and appurtenances than one ought to accumulate in a mere year's run but somehow does. I drove away from my greatest success which engendered my greatest Paradox – that is, my greatest misery – the rat race my father warned me of when I first told him I wanted to go on the stage, bringing us full circle to Truth, Serendipity, and the Oxford Enigma which, with the insight yielded by all these historically – recorded, diary – validated facts – we are finally about to solve! But spare me, I beg you, another moment!

How much all of us in the public eye lose by misrepresentation I do not know. What it has done to our name out there in the misty vales of celebrity we can only guess. All we can do is repeat the words of James Cagney, who, when asked why he had written his autobiography said: 'I wanted to put the record straight.'

Part three

The Singular Solution to the Enigma

1

The Projection Curve

ow we come to it, the nitty-gritty, the crunch, the moment of truth, the puzzle-breaker we have been seeking to crack as we surveyed the first seven years of my career, from the beginning of 1953 to the middle of 1961. And all measured against the concept of Personal Praise, and the Enigma of its absence.

Was my account of the seven-year leap from LSE to *Oliver!* perhaps so closely detailed that some of you have already sussed out the solution to the Enigma? Better, have any of you formulated your own theory or improved on mine, in which case more power to your intellectual elbow, *you* can write the book, *I'll* take the royalty, *you* pay the tax!

Failing all these – here at last is what it's all about!

The name of the book was originally *The Projection Curve*, then abbreviated to *Pro-Curve*, which was the working title that popped straight into my head but which seemed to me to give the game away too easily. Why? Surely the instant you saw *Projection Curve* you thought of the projection aperture whence light dances on a cinema screen! Correct? Well, it isn't!

Here I have to confess that the singular solution to the

Enigma unravelled itself quite suddenly in Oxford at 6pm on Saturday, 20th October, 2001. I could have written it straight down, but cerebral temptations may have led me to the big mistake . . . I *thought* about it. Even worse, I *thought* about it *before* I *wrote* it. And so, what with the thinking about it and the writing about it, and other commitments that would insist on coming along, it has taken seven years to get this far! The truth is, every time I sat down to write I got a job.

So let us get it sorted. My agent, Janet Glass, had come up from London to see the matinee of *Comedians* and after it we'd gone out to a less than Lucullan feast in a nearby eatery for me to pile on ergs for the next show and for her to pick apart the last one. Janet wasn't terribly impressed – she didn't think the production merited going into town. That was a reasonable assumption, since the next performance was the last and nobody had mentioned a last-minute transfer any more than they had mentioned *me*. So – which was more to the point – what was wrong with my performance? She had come all this way to see her client, *me*, playing what might have been misinterpreted as the *leading part*, and had not even mentioned me, apart from a slightly inaudible comment when she came back to my dressing-room. Why, it's 'Thank you, Mr Moody' all over again!

All over again, the dreaded lurgi of indifference had contaminated even my own team. But there was more! She didn't think it would have been worth my while going into town with it. And as I chewed over my steak and what she had said, it occurred to me that however hard I had tried, *I was no better than the rest*!

How could that be, when I had put so much into the part? I'd worked on tape, I'd worked the Manchester accent over and over with the dialect coach, I *was* a traditional Mancunian Comedian in the flesh! I felt I'd added to Jimmy Jewel's deep-rooted truth and natural acting skill all my extra years of character-creation, building Eddie Waters into something more than just a realistically-observed Northern comic, acting *from the gut*! In the final powerful scene, I played the pietà of the soul in torment, the man who suffered the pain of the victims of the Nazi camps, suffering with them when he roared at the callous, cold-blooded Price who knew and felt nothing of that hideous era. I was giving so much, I was bursting at the seams of Eddie Waters! I felt that I was adding histrionic height to the character, just as Olivier added his own brand of theatrical power to *The Entertainer*, pushing it beyond naturalism into heroic romanticism.

FAGIN   Heroic what?

MOODY   Somebody speak? (MOODY *looks round, sees nothing and continues*) I felt that I was giving my own brand of novelty, adding creative touches that had, in other work, been met with considerable Personal Praise. Just as I had managed to find the measured wit and wicked chicanery for the Governor of Buenos Aires in *Candide*, and the endless invention and unpredictability for Fagin in *Oliver!*

FAGIN   *You* found Fagin? Chutzpah!

MOODY   But what I *felt*, was obviously not coming over! Where was all that energy and Truth and invention going *this* time?

FAGIN   Where was all that energy and truth and invention going *this* time? well, if it wasnt coming over then surely it had to be going upwards or downwards or backwards or even bloody-well *sideways*!

MOODY   Who said *sideways*? Who *is* that?

FAGIN   Your old mate! Fagin!

And with that, the face of Fagin appeared in the dressing-room monitor, stroking his beard with the deep-thinking air of a demented professor.

MOODY   What in tarnation are you doing in there?

FAGIN   Sorry to disturb your moment of sagacious exploration, my dear, but I'd listened to enough of your multi-syllabic twaddle! Firstly, I didn't know what you were talking about because I didn't see your flipping play – er – *Comedians*! Secondly, I didn't understand half your long words and I was fed up with looking 'em up in a dictionary!

MOODY   What would you do with a dictionary?

FAGIN   Words, my dear, lovely words, infinite usages! I 'ad a dictionary propping shut the door of me privy before you were born! And my advice to you is 'simplify'. Too many long words, you won't sell half a dozen!

MOODY   Stephen Hawkins wrote *A Brief History of Time*, a book that nobody understood after page 29, and that was a best seller.

FAGIN   So suddenly you're Stephen Hawkins?

MOODY   Of course not. (*Thinks*) But I can imitate him. Speak slow into a glass tumbler, with an American accent! (FAGIN *chuckles*) Enough of this, where was I? Oh, yes, lunching with my agent on 20th October, 2001. I was staring into space and thinking about 'sideways'. If I was no better than the rest, then something was siphoning off the vital juices that nourished my pride in craftsmanship, draining off my energy, working silently and insidiously and almost certainly *sideways* against my actor's drive to send energy *forwards* to the audience. Was this what my former dresser Suli meant when she expected so much more of me in Exeter? Was this what Vernon and other friends meant when their praise had all the enthusiasm of an afterthought? And why didn't Janet think it would be worth *my* while to go into Town? Somebody was certainly trying to tell me something! What was it I couldn't see?

FAGIN   I thought you just saw.

MOODY   You have a ready wit, sir!

FAGIN   Thank you.

MOODY   Let me know when it's ready! (FAGIN *cackles*) Come on, if you're so smart, what was the next logical step as the clock ticked steadily towards the penny-drop at 6pm on that Saturday?

FAGIN   Penny-drop? I dunno what you're talking about. Keep it simple!

MOODY   *(controlling himself)* Very well. Reasoning as steadily as possible and moving step by simple step, here we go following the trail that leads to our ultimate destination, the Projection Curve!

FAGIN   What's a Projection Curve?

MOODY   The Projection Curve is the line that joins equidistant focal points towards which vocal strength and personality are projected.

FAGIN   Ay, yay, yay! Who wrote that?

MOODY   I did! New ideas need new words, open a fresh page in your brain, old man.

FAGIN   Enough with the old man! I understand very well about the bolstering of new theories with novel terminologies. Where would the Freudian be without his Unconscious and his Ego and his Id?

MOODY   *(mouth agape)* What? How do you know that?

FAGIN   Born in 1838, laddie, I've had plenty of time to read. You'd be surprised who comes to my soirées. Now, go on, and keep it simple.

MOODY   Right! Firstly, from the beginning of this book I have reminded you again and again about the Oxford Enigma, i.e. the lack of Personal Praise for my work – our work – in *Comedians*. The rest of the company dismissed it, I persisted. It was more than my feeling that the least of such praise is necessary for encouragement. It was in fact a signal, a clear warning, as a smell of burning is the first sign of an incinerated steak. But what was it a warning of? If you are a worthwhile artist who cares to enchant his fellow man or woman, you will seek until you find the answer.

FAGIN   OK, I'm seeking.

MOODY   Good! Now then, if *Comedians* does not move viewers to Personal Praise it would suggest you are not delivering the goods. Ask yourself: is the performance all on one level? Does it lack the kind of impact that audiences have come to expect? In a word, does it lack Full Frontal Impact (or Impact Acting), which sends out enormous power with effortless skill and communicates all levels of emotional depth? Why is this impact less than it should be, in *Comedians*?

FAGIN   Tell me.

MOODY   It's pretty obvious that the frontal-seeking theatrical energy that gives a performance its impact is somehow leaking away, and we already have the clue that in *Comedians* the energy seems to be going sideways. And here is where, not surprisingly, the director has exerted his influence on the production; here is an extreme form of Theatrical Ensemble where, by focusing so intently on each other, we are sending the mental and verbal energy sideways, from actor to actor, thus reducing the impact of the production. And that was why I was no better than the rest, and why none of us was good enough to go into Town. And that was when the concept of the Projection Curve was born!

FAGIN   What was that again?

MOODY   As I've said, the Projection Curve, or Pro-Curve, is the line that joins equidistant focal points towards which vocal strength and personality are projected. Thus, an opera singer in the Arena Verona will project his voice to the focal point at the outer wall of the arena and also think himself out to that focal point, so that his entire talent and vocal power and personality reach even the almond-sellers at the farthest reaches of the mighty building. Another singer of similar qualities will project to the same distance so that they share a projection curve. If the curve is too small, fewer people are reached with less force. It's where the artist decides he belongs, where he places his voice and his personality, which enables him to achieve maximum impact (Full Frontal Impact).

FAGIN   (*in pain*)   Please! Just for me, instead of a plate-licking blow-out of long words and short meanings, try to give a concrete example of real people in real places – someone we know.

MOODY   Like you.

FAGIN   Me?

MOODY   With a load of boys?

FAGIN   Can't think of a thing.

MOODY   Singing a song? Here! Now! An example!

FAGIN   Like what?

MOODY   *Pick a Pocket*?

FAGIN   I've heard of that. Right! (*He claps his hands*

	together) Let's show Oliver how to do it, my dears! (*Hums*) Rum, tum, tum, tum! Rum, tum tum tum! I'm in the middle, a dozen little villains all around me. Now, boys, remember to include each other but play to the front. Never turn your back – or side!
BOYS	Or backside! (*Yelling*) On the audience!
FAGIN	What do we call it?
BOYS	*Frontality*!
FAGIN	(*sings*) *In this life, one thing counts.*
	In the bank, large amounts . . .

As I sing and move and act, I stand on stage facing forwards, punching every ounce of energy up and out to the gods. I am giving the highest level of frontal-seeking theatrical energy, there is no leakage of energy, and I and the boys are aiming our Projection Curve – or Pro-Curve – entirely to the gods. And because of this, when we finish the show we will receive considerable Personal Praise!

Right! Now for an example that starts the same – there we are, punching every ounce of energy up and out to the gods. But this time we have energy leakage from a whole host of things ('Subverted Pro-Curves' I s'pose you'd call them): a hangover from the First Night celebrations, fatigue, stress, illness, preoccupations (that unpaid tax bill or Penalty Notice lingering on the mantelpiece – particularly intrusive if you're playing *Hamlet* and you find yourself saying: 'To pay or not to pay?' Yipes!), loss of confidence, under-rehearsal, turning the energy sideways (as in your excessive Ensemble), and not uncommonly, directorial indulgences. Result: lack of impact, no Personal Praise.

In sum, nobody should go on stage without a full understanding of the Pro-Curve and control of his theatrical energy!

MOODY Well, I must say I am amazed at *your* understanding and control of theatrical energy.

FAGIN Well, either you got it or you ain't! Now I have to
go. Got a lunch appointment with Charlie – er –
Mr Dickens, and Mr Brownlow has invited me
and the missus over for tea. Life goes on. Adieu!

And with a skip and an entrechat, old Fagin was gone.

These Subverted Pro-Curves, or negative counter-forces,
offshoots and complications which divert the actor's energy
away from its legitimate target – the audience – are
responsible for the public saying: 'He's walking through the
show and I paid £50 a ticket!', or the director shouting over
the Tannoy: 'I watched the show tonight and you were all a
bloody shambles!' or everybody saying: 'Thank you, Mr
Moody.'

There are, I suppose, as many Subverted Pro-Curves as
there are human weaknesses. Summer seasons are particularly susceptible to the sun soaking up energy, and an
actor's good day on the beach is a guarantee of a bad night in
the theatre. Take care when playing seaside resorts or when
the ozone relaxes your throat and reduces your projection to
a wheeze, you'll wonder where you placed your bel canto!

But probably the greatest professional interference with the
Projection Curve comes from the confusions and mis-
directions of experiments with formal strategy and tactics.
The works of Shakespeare are fair game for every
improvisational young genius eager to make his name. Just
recently, I had a letter from an actor who had been directed to
play Trinculo in *The Tempest* as a transvestite book-keeper!
One way, I suppose, of playing a jester. Hate to think what
that genius did with Caliban. A bisexual waitress? 'Tea, sir?
One hump or two?'

Many years ago I played Autolycus in *The Winter's Tale* on
television, and Don Taylor, the director, fresh down from

university, had written a bitterly anti-romantic thesis on that beautifully romantic play, and he didn't want to waste it. So instead of sylvan glades and babbling brooks we inhabited a world of metal brambles and tin trees. Well, I suppose that was anti-romantic. And indeed, some of the actors went for the tin-tack spine of the director's thesis. I was too green to know better in my first Shakespeare and played it for laughs, and lovely Patrick McNee played Steed. I wasn't too clear about the others. In the end, the romantic writing won by a length, Shakespeare defeated Don Taylor, and Love Conquered All. But the experience was like putting salt in your tea. Biting the skin as well as the orange. We were all too busy being clever and experimental and even in the intimacy of television half the power and intent had gone into the gimmick. The result was no better than the consensus on Sean Holmes's treatment of *Comedians*!

Sean's very particular style of direction set up (full strength) Ibsen's Fourth Wall, with the cast projecting their voices and personalities sideways, thereby locking themselves within the proscenium frame, never daring to come out. We were never actually told not to dare, but it was always there, the overwhelming feeling that one was held in a vice, never daring to make a move or utter a syllable that had not been directorially stated and restated. So what we had was an extreme form of Theatrical Ensemble, where the restraint on one's freedom was imposed, oddly enough, by one's peers. The result was that we were playing to each other, feeding each other the Truth of each scene, and cutting off our audience from it. The world we now lived in had little meaning for the audience outside it. No wonder the lack of Personal Praise!

Normally, a Theatrical Ensemble is any established group of managers, directors, designers and actors working together on equal terms out of concern for their communal welfare and artistic growth. They agree, ideally, to:

Equal salary.

Equal billing.

Equal publicity.

Equal casting, i.e. King Lear one week, a spear-carrier the next. (More or less.)

Equal concern for each other's careers. (More or less.)

And anything else you can think up to remind you that 'ensemble' is French for 'together'.

It isn't long before the Company comes well before the individuals. As Michael Boyd, Artistic Director of the Royal Shakespeare Company, said, 'It imposes homogeneity on a group of talents that would be better celebrated in their vivid individuality.'

The Ensemble can also be Positive or Negative. A Positive Ensemble works together for the benefit of the *audience*, who enjoy the skill and polish that come from long-shared teamwork. Though I found fault with the energy projection in *Comedians*, I admired the well-knit production – but what a long, long way from the Revues, where although the eight or ten of us were in principle all equal, with alphabetical billing, the senior members got the single numbers which won the notices and the kudos. And Ronnie Stevens directed the sketches then turned us loose – no heavy-handed drilling here, we were free agents, licensed to do our own thing. We worked together but remained competitive, building together into a dynamic – not static – ensemble of mutual creativity.

A Negative Ensemble, on the other hand, works together for the benefit of the *cast*, who indulge in private jokes to make each other 'corpse' on stage in order to relieve the boredom of a long run. (Purists will not accept that a genuine pile-up does occasionally happen, but I have to say I've succumbed to a few. In *Fine Fettle*, the Benny Hill show in which Vivienne Martin was the brilliantly funny female lead and sang *'I'm No Good as a Scarecrow 'Cos I Love Crows'* – a number I wrote for her – a giant cart-horse was brought on stage. All went well until it mistook the set for an equine toilet and, being a well-trained animal, delivered a hundredweight on the spot.)

FAGIN   *(popping in again and cackling)* That's what you call a real pile-up.

MOODY   The laugh lasted all through the clean-up by a team of deadpan stagehands and into the next number with Shani Wallis singing a love song where all the words seemed to reflect the horse's dastardly deed, but fortunately I can't remember the words.

FAGIN   I can! She sang *'Now look what you've done'* and *'It's not my love you're leaving around, baby!'*

MOODY   You can't write lines like that.

FAGIN   You can't remember them!

MOODY   Anyway, an Ensemble may work well enough on film or television where the camera moves in and takes what it wants, but on stage the audience is doomed to Death by Sameness, everything equally flat. Drilling the cast into a herd of well-trained zombies can never be what theatre is about! And that was why I was no better than the rest! And that was why none of us were good enough to go into Town! And that was when the concept of the Projection Curve . . .

FAGIN   *(fed up)* You've already told us that Goodnight! *(he goes)*

MOODY   *(oblivious)* . . . was born.

The Projection Curve may be extended beyond its theatrical application to include all kinds of interpersonal contact: politicians, teachers, the clergy, sergeant-majors, fairground hustlers, fathers of the bride, and anyone, professional or amateur, who communicates through any kind of space from a dinner table to a parade ground. Just recently I listened to the Head of Department in a local school addressing an audience of parents. She could see there were a couple of hundred people there, but she addressed them on a projection curve that barely dribbled over her top lip. Nobody muttered 'Speak up!', but she was followed soon after by man who aimed his projection curve at the back of the hall and was consequently perfectly audible.

There are examples of poor projection on stage that one would never believe possible. Two of America's finest film actors gave performances on the London stage that barely came over the footlights. George C. Scott in *Three Sisters*, and Al Pacino in *American Buffalo* – Top Lip Pro-Curves, the pair of them! Great actors talking into cotton wool. Students were baffled, even following the play in their books. Why? Because Scott and Pacino are film actors. So many years of projecting in whispers and growls to throat mikes or overhead booms that they forgot, or were not warned – where was the director? – that on stage they needed to rev up the ergs and place their voices at the back wall of the auditorium.

The exact position and the exact Projection Curve at which the speaker succeeds or fails can be calibrated with the following focal points. (The grading is generally boosted these days by minute microphones stuck in the most undignified places. I hate them! Behind the ear, beneath the wig, where else? Lord help the bald man with no ears! But the advice of Stella Adler, New York acting maven, still applies: 'Actors walk like gods upon the earth; fill the stage with size!' Which means 'Belt it out, even in a stage whisper, and let it fill the whole magic shell.)

(1) TOP LIP. A Pro-Curve so weak that it barely trickles over the top lip and drips silently to the floor. The effect ranges from silence to a murmur and a bad-tempered audience. One may also say: 'His Pro-Curve barely reaches his beard.'

(2) HANDSTRETCH. An arm's length from the resonant cavities and just as useless unless you employ sign language.

(3) ORCHESTRA PIT OR FRONT STALLS. A few lucky people in the front row might hear something, the rest think they are watching a mime.

(4) BACK STALLS. A reasonable projection which motivates the Circle and above to pay for a better seat.

(5) CIRCLE. Nearly everybody is satisfied.

(6) THE GODS. Only possible with a Full Frontal Impact Projection Curve.

You expect to see the greatest at the old *Night of a 100 Stars*, and the last one I went to certainly had them. Olivier, Leigh and Danny Kaye tore 'em up, Noel Coward proved himself as ever the Master, but who stole the show? Who came on and made Full Frontal Impact twice the size of anybody else's? Dear old Frankie Howerd! He sauntered up to the front stage and just stood there. He didn't even look at his mark. He didn't need one. His face was twice as big as real life, he radiated confidence, and possessed a projection curve that went zooming to the back of the gods and straight out for a close-up on the Hubble.

'Ladies . . . and . . . Gentle . . . men . . . What? . . . No . . . yes . . . now then . . .' That's all he said. So it was hardly the words! It was Frankie placing himself right in the lap of every ripple he projected to the audience. Zowie! The Full Frontal Impact Projection Curve! Such power is met mainly in Opera, Music Hall, Rock Concert and Cabaret, where the artist is in total, facial, full-frontal contact with each member of his audience. And if that seems a bit near the mark, so be it.

There is the famous tale of an interviewer asking probably the greatest screen actor of all time, Spencer Tracy, for his advice on acting in film. Tracy replied at once: 'Learn your lines and keep to your marks!' No one recorded the interviewer's reaction, but he must have expected at least a paragraph – even a book – on the Art of Film Acting. But when you do the acting, believe me, it's enough! Only if you know and understand your lines one hundred percent, and are word perfect out of respect for the screenwriter's skill – and only if you have rehearsed the scene so thoroughly that the action can be marked out by a piece of gaffer tape – only then can you give yourself to that wondrous repose, that awesome ownership of the screen, that was so typical of the great Tracy. Even if he did make a point of looking down at his mark when he approached camera, pausing, and quite casually looking up. In his own time. As on stage, Pro-Curve impact depends on the placing of voice and personality.

2

The Equation But Not Quite Einstein

We have used the Pro-Curve tools to diagnose the problem that dogged us in *Comedians*, but there is one more analytic tool to consider – an Equation. We don't have one! But every bona fide theory has an Equation to encapsulate it so why shouldn't Pro-Curve? It may have no purpose except to add methodological clout to our research, but you don't have a Rolls Royce without a Spirit of Ecstasy on the bonnet! Pro-Curve must have a Spirit of Equation!

So let us look at the most famous equation in history and ask ourselves, 'How dared a humble patent clerk, third class, in the Bern Patent Office (1905) presume to send a paper on some Antick Theory of Relativity, complete with equation, $E = mc^2$, to the formidable *Annalen der Physik* and expect it to be accepted?' I haven't an ounce of math (as the Americans, Guardians of the World and the Moral High Ground, so nicely put it) to compute such an equation, but these days equations are not all mathematical or quantified, they may rather be statements of relationships between *qualities*, a kind of 'one goes up, the other goes down' sort of thing, something a mathless dunderhead like me might be able to manage. Something rather like dear old Albert's Equation – in fact, what better Equation to build on than Einstein's Special Theory of Relativity! Especially since his theory is to do with the creation of energy and Pro-Curve is to do with the projection of theatrical energy. Even Personal Praise is a kind of energy, and the denial of it is nothing less than negative energy (the first theatrical Black Hole?).

If in Physics: $E = mc^2$ (that is, Energy = Mass x The Speed of Light squared), why not in Theatre: $Et = mt \times PC^2$ (that is, Theatrical Energy = Character Mass x Pro-Curve squared)? Which is to say, the Energy of the Actor on Stage equals the Quality of his Performing Skills times Optimum Projection Curve squared.

Thus our Equation comes down to this: if the character is fully developed and powerfully drawn, with exemplary acting, dancing, singing and other skills (mt); and if the Pro-Curve is at its optimum distance so that the performance comes fully across to the entire audience (PC^2), the total Theatrical Energy (Et) rises to Full Frontal Impact Acting.

Conversely, a poorly drawn character and a misplaced Pro-Curve will reduce the impact of Theatrical Energy to performance without presence. Even worse, taken purely on the surface, these flawed qualities will result in a misinterpretation and misplaced critique of the play.

We now have an equation that links the elements of Theatrical Energy and presents them in a convenient shorthand form that allows us to apply the theory and judge whether it succeeds or fails. So, let us put one or two of the trickiest moments under the microscope.

First, the Trial Run. I was 16 and it was my first-ever appearance. Somehow I had managed to fiddle myself into a talent show at the local hall. I had prepared a pretty good impression of George Formby playing 'When I'm Cleaning Windows' on his uke. The moment arrived and I plunked my uke and began to sing and totally dried. I stood and looked at the invisible audience for some time, and walked off. In total silence. Was I no good? What does the Pro-Curve analysis say?

(1) *Pro-Curve*: less than Top Lip. Totally *zero*.
(2) *Counter-Forces*:
    (a) Personal. I had never been on stage before and in my total panic the lines went, the voice went and I went.
    (b) Professional. Confidence and memory non-existent.
    (c) Director. There was no director we can blame
(3) *Equation*: $Et = mt \times PC^2$
$$0/10 = \text{Good Impression of Formby} \times \text{Top Lip (zero)}$$
(4) *Summation:* I was well rehearsed, and facing the audience full on, thus gaining all the advantages of a Full Frontal Impact, but lacking any Projection Curve I managed to subvert every morsel of its energy! They didn't react to me because I didn't exist for them. I had swallowed all my words, my personality and myself. The Character (mt) was good, the Pro-Curve (PC^2) was kaput!

So there was of course no Theatrical Energy, no Personal Praise, and no Enigma then, because at that age I thought an Enigma was something you did in a toilet.

Let's look again at the *Vagabond Student* scena in the light of Pro-Curve analysis. And I don't mean Nina's blissful remark: 'I sat out front the other day and it seemed to me you all think you're very funny'! That is all about the 'pro' who, drunk on laughter, thinks he's a very funny person. And shows it! And ay, there's the rub. By showing his vanity he sets the audience against him and they find it hard to laugh at a preening pomp.

But Pro-Curve analysis has no discourse with vanity. It seeks solutions rather in terms of *Energy*. It identifies the problem as bored actors in a long run seeking an outlet for their stale spirits by changing voices and business *to make each other laugh*! No thought here for *them out there*, paying for tickets, this is all for them up here, looking to have a little fun!

What's wrong with that, if it's funny?

Simply that by playing together in what we have called Negative Ensemble, the company is projecting its Energy sideways, and not aiming for Full Frontal Impact. So when rehearsal is called to put it right, we don't need the director to tell us to cut the funny stuff and go back to the original, we need a Pro-Curve practitioner who tells us to keep the new stuff if it works for the show, and go back to playing it with frontality to those nice people who have made a special trip here for the very reasonable purpose of being entertained!

Summation: They stopped laughing at us because we swallowed half our energy sideways in Negative Ensemble.

If that sounds a little sharp-edged, allow me a little *mea culpa*. I have been one of the worst offenders, especially in cabaret. I've always had a great time with musicians in every night club in the West End, from Felix King and Phil Phillips to Sydney Simone and Edmundo Ros, leading at the Astor, Churchills, the Colony, the Coconut Grove, the Savoy and Dorchester, and on bad nights I knew I could depend on the deep, rusty rumble of laughter from the boys sitting behind me and pouncing on every ad lib and misfire. So sometimes, when there were few people in, I played to them. A prime example of Negative Ensemble! I even played to them once when the house was full – but that was a fullness of Japanese tourists who didn't understand a word. I've found the best laughers have been musicians and the CID – sharp wits, never miss a trick! But in any case there is no problem in cabaret, where the Full Frontal Impact Pro-Curve is unsurpassed. *You* are there entirely for *them*! There is no entertainment mode to match it in the world!

3
An Epiphany — But Not Quite

The discovery of the Projection Curve was really very exciting. I might have described it as an epiphany, but I wasn't in mystical mood. No, it was the sheer relief of finding a reason for the peculiar lack of Personal Praise, and that Personal Praise does have significance, that gave me such a lift. But I didn't mention it to anyone. I needed time to take it in. Janet took a train back to London and I went back to the theatre and put my feet up in the dressing-room and looked, as always, at my script.

Performing in *Comedians* after the moment of truth was quite peculiar. At first I felt no different, then I had the peculiar sense of being inside a goldfish bowl, enclosed by the play. But then the awareness of entrapment had me looking up to the deep back doubles of the theatre, I fished for my new space right out there in the back row — what am I saying, it was my *old* space, where I've always lived, encompassing the entire audience. There they are, my people — the old feelings of warmth and love returning — welcome home to LSE! How *dare* anyone take all this away from me, this is my world, these are my people, my God, I'm still not getting any laughs, but at least now we're *home*, on with the ad libs and the shtick, it's just a matter of time.

Not really thinking too much about the Projection Curve, only the fact that the entire house has opened up to welcome me, that wonderful special darkness of the auditorium, my peculiar ability to see way back into the stalls. 'Who's in tonight, Ron?' somebody asks. 'The Aga Khan is asleep in the front row!' I reply. I'm settling down, now, embracing the whole theatre, growing in size, watch out, Frankie Howerd, the big man cometh!

The last scene of the play with the Indian who wants to join Eddie's class and instantly revives his enthusiasm, is a belter. There were always a few laughs here, but now it is what I always wanted – the funny man who *was*, becoming the funny man who *is*. The laughter sets off a warm buzz in the viscera, it breeds more, the funny feeling feeds the power to make more laughter. Oh, I wish we were only starting the run! We take our calls with a feeling of triumph, if this splendour had struck before, we might well have transferred. But I don't feel any sense of defeat, the discovery of the Projection Curve has made everything worthwhile.

I will sleep on it, decide what to do with it. And forearmed by this bizarre experience, I will certainly never allow it to happen again. I have got back my artistic autonomy, to hell with fancy names and sprauncy titles and pretty ladies who say: 'Thank you, Mr Moody.' I'm in charge of my God-given talent, and I'll work *with* you but I bloody well won't work *under* you!

I'm always last out of the dressing-room on the last night because I take so long packing my make-up case.

I walk out of the seedy Stage Door into the seedy alley-way with the cobblestones and the entrance to an even seedier pub, and corkscrew round the corner into the more salubrious air of Beaumont Street, a few yards from the theatre bar, packed with patrons spilling out of the door. I normally pass by and go straight to the Randolph for a beer and a snack, but

I have to find out if something has happened tonight, even if I'm lugging a make-up box filled with fifty years of clutter.

I don't need to.

A young couple standing drinking at the door see me, their faces light up, they hold out their programmes.

'Wonderful show, Mr Moody!'

'You were great!'

'Thank you.'

I sign their programmes, decide to skip the bar because I'm tired and will be leaving Oxford tomorrow, and I go into the Randolph and up to my room and finish off the little box of chocolates shaped like a mortarboard.

How idiotic!

Comedians ends just as I am about to start work on it.

Never mind.

I sprawl out on the bed, ring down for a Ploughman's and a 1664 and begin to make notes on the projection Curve.

THE END
(but not quite)

Postlude

We have examined the first seven years of my career. Did we need to do that? Couldn't we have gone straight to Part Three and made this book a short theoretical pamphlet? No, because I wanted to do more, I wanted to show how a career in theatre begins and develops, and how the actor faces and handles the exhilaration and despair and the confusion and '*Eureka, I have found it!*' moments that typify the working pattern of an actor's life. I wanted to explore the enigmas and conundrums and tantalizing brain-teasers that pop up at every turn.

The Projection Curve weaves vertebraically (I think I made that word up!) through those first years of theatrical activity, always below the surface, never quite spotted. But isn't that the great thing about 'the ever-whirling wheels of change'? – it may be only when something is discovered that you realise it's been there all the time!

Our old friend Truth demands the addition of one little *arrière-pensée*. I have tried to leave it out of the book, only to find that if I do, I simply cannot get it out of my head. Perhaps because so many secrets have leaked from the pages of my diary, things that I wish I'd never written (but enjoy so much when I read back!). Awfully rude things that might have been better left out in the interests of preserving the pristine images of decency and fairplay and other illusions you may still have about me

I have tried in the book to patch things up with Georgia, to console myself with the possibility that the intensity of our feelings may have spurred us on to efforts that made the show even better. My abiding sadness is the one-sided feud that I certainly didn't want and to this day don't understand. What did I do to bring that on? What did I do that I hadn't been doing for nearly a year? If just one person at the helm had had a little more diplomacy, we might have resolved the problem and made *Oliver!* a hugely happy as well as a hugely successful show. It's a little late now, but not too late to say: 'Sorry, Georgia, sorry, my dear. I never wanted to hurt you, I just wanted to make people laugh. And I want you to know that you were always the greatest Nancy! Even in my angriest moments I was in awe of your powerful talent. If it was my fault, please forgive me.'

Well, there we are. A few apologies, stored up for far too many years, a few regrets, as if doing it again would be any different.

Peter Coe and I worked together so many times afterwards that whatever we thought about each other, our mutual respect and dislike were never questioned.

Special thanks here for Sean Holmes (now Artistic Director of the Lyric Hammersmith), whose directorial methods launched me on this flight of theoretical theatrical fancy. If I misunderstood your intentions, Sean, then please accept my apologies for a serendipitous error. PS If you've got a play coming up at the Lyric, I'm free!

Thank you, Vivienne Martin, for your continuous inspiration and your marvellous knack of guiding me back on track when I lost my way. (Incidentally, where were you during *Comedians*? With you around it might have had the mischief – and the laughter – which were so sadly lacking.)

Albery was Albery, Bobby Lewis was Bobby Lewis, some

people have to be who they are, and we need them that way or who's left to dislike? In my early days in show business I had a hate list which I found motivated me much better than gooey old luvvies. One of my favourite hates was Lou Grade (I loved Bernie and Leslie), then I worked with Lou on a Barbara Cartland film, *Ghost in Monte Carlo*, and he was like a dear old uncle to me!

Which brings me to Lionel Bart. Why did he get so angry with me? I just thought that his huge success had gone to his head (but tell me, pray, to which part of the anatomy is it supposed to go?). I may not have given him everything he wanted in Fagin, but I brought to it a bundle of creative variables accumulated from the seven years of creative pioneering that came before. And then I got the letter – or rather, a very old-fashioned duplicate of a type-written letter dated 26th March, 1968, from Lionel Bart to John Box, Production Designer on the film of *Oliver!* It was sent to me by Barbara Evans, Curator of the Lionel Bart Archives, and here's the bit that really surprised me. Bart writes:

> '. . . in my viewing of the fine rough cut (or should it be called "the rough fine cut"), the most rewarding moments for me were Ron Moody's performance more or less consistently, together with the moments when your own personal magic stood out a mile.'

That's all. Only one line! But a heart-warming compliment, even if he had to kvetch a bit with 'more or less consistently'. So Lionel was happy after all. A bit like my Dad, never told me I was 'great' but boy, did he brag to his mates!

So all is well in the world of *Oliver!*, the Paradox fades to nothing, the happy show is happy in its roots and ever will be. Good on you, Li

The Postlude was categorically intended to be the very end of the book, finis – genug – I'm outta-here-type finality.
But like one of those candles that keep re-igniting on a quirky birthday cake, the book kept refusing to end!

The Last Word

Tried, Tested and Quite, Quite Proven

The boy was no longer 16. He was a man of 86. Clearly, time had passed. He had a wash of wet lettuce about the chops, boasting a wealth of pills and creative medication. Never done this before – well, only inside his locked study, entirely by himself, facing the mirror, singing *Pick a Pocket*, wearing the threadbare mittens he had broken in on the original *Oliver!* run and tucked away for a rainy day. He was still missing cues and verses as he used to do in the '50s, fifty years ago. If you're gonna have a lousy memory, have a lousy memory, and that's what he had when he first tried to learn it all.

Only thing was, he couldn't do the moves now, dammit; couldn't do the clown-walks-on-the-spot, the pas de basque, the entrechat – no question that if he did, something would snap! True, not so long ago in Canterbury at a 400-strong Community Theatre, he had warmed up slowly and by the end was *pas de basquing* all round the stage. And his voice was still on top form – bel canto, lieder, Jolson, Astaire, you name it – and you can sing without moving, so remember the old trick, if you can't do it, don't show it!

Well, here he was, backstage again. Wednesday, 30th June, 2010. The impresario Cameron Mackintosh had decided to celebrate the 50th Anniversary of *Oliver!* Fifty years since the first night, but he remembered that First Night as if it were just happening. As for being backstage, this time it didn't seem to be totally deserted, it was packed to the wings with cast! And there was no need to fiddle his way in, the Great Mackintosh himself had invited him as Guest of Honour, the first and most original Fagin! He had been met by two very pretty young dancers, not in stomach-melting tutus but nonetheless exquisite, to escort him on. But he made it clear to them that they mustn't look as if they were carrying him, they were *partners* dancing on to *I'd Do Anything* – and hey presto! – ol' Doctor Greasepaint he done waved his wand, and Moody done fergit he had an aching bunion and a thick head from the summer heat, and strutted his turn to the lectern, *supporting* the two dollybirds as if the days of chivalry had never left him, singing '*Would you rob a shop?*'

The audience rose as one man. If that worries you, they rose as one woman. Anyway, they rose, 2,500 people, clapping and cheering our hero, who suddenly realised, as if he could ever forget it, that they were his people and what was coming over the footlights and the chain-mail clad orchestra pit were waves and waves and waves of LOVE! He had returned to them after fifty years and they loved him for it!

AND THAT'S WHEN HE HAD THE IDEA! AFTER SEVEN YEARS OF FORMULATING PROJECTION-CURVE THEORY, SURELY NOW WAS THE TIME TO TEST IT! HE WAS GOING TO DO THIS ANNIVERSARY SPEECH ON FULL FRONTAL IMPACT. HE WAS GOING TO SELL IT TO THE GODS, AND PUNCH ALL HIS ENERGY RIGHT OUT THERE

TO THE BACK OF THE TOP SHELF! NOTHING SIDEWAYS HERE!

No longer blinded by the spotlights spouting lava, he could see the entire audience in the great cavern of the auditorium, all the monsters that certainly lurked there and bought tickets. He began his speech, admitting he was deeply disturbed by the whole experience because he was doing it for *nothing*! Not getting a sausage! A salt-beef sandwich even? A pickle maybe?

He talked of Bart's melodies, ranging from Music Hall to Yiddisha Borscht Belt. He told how he managed to remember the order of verses in *Reviewing the Situation*. And he described that incredible First Night at the New Theatre when they all shouted 'Author!' and Lionel Bart walked out of the wings, onto the stage, and into musical theatre history.

He then paid tribute to Cameron Mackintosh for keeping the musical alive, and finished with a barrage of funny toasts.

As he was about to take his bow, a small boy cheeky enough to be the Dodger thrust himself beneath Moody's guard and said:

'Sing *Pick a Pocket*, please?'

'No!'

'Ooooh, sing *Pick a Pocket*?'

'I've forgotten the words!'

The boy burst into tears – there was a general clamour! Moody looked at the boobela, relented and yielded. He sang all six verses, sharing with Russ Abbott, the incumbent Fagin (what great fun that man is!), and the audience.

And not once did he dry, stone cold dead in de market, because the director had installed a very large crib with all the first lines of *Pick a Pocket* inside the lectern, and even Moody couldn't miss that!

Another huge standing ovation.

There had been something different about this performance – what was it?

After the show, at the reception in the Grand Saloon, Personal Praise was an understatement – the compliments were gigantic! There, that sense of – what? – again! The old man sat down. His wife Therese was glowing with pride, even his hard-to-please sons had to admit the old man had something – a queue of pretty young girls with very short skirts lined up to get his autograph! What *was* all this? He'd only done half an hour, not a full show.

And then came the key to the last of the Enigmas.

The grandfather of one of the cast had a question for me. 'Mr Moody, did you feel like a *bigger* star tonight?'

Strange question. I hadn't felt like a 'big star' since the days of the film, why should I feel more like one tonight? And then I thought about it and I said, 'Yes.' I *did*! From the moment I went on and aimed my Pro-Curve at the gods with Full Frontal Impact.

The Projection Curve worked!

I had grown in size, I had reached my peak!

TRIED, TESTED AND QUITE, QUITE PROVEN.